ARRANGING
ROSES

ARRANGING
ROSES

Inspirational ideas using fresh
and dried flowers

Consultant editor: Emma Gray

HERMES
HOUSE

First published in 1999 by Hermes House

Hermes House is an imprint of
Anness Publishing Limited
Hermes House
88–89 Blackfriars Road
London SE1 8HA

Published in the USA by Hermes House
Anness Publishing Inc., 27 West 20th Street, New York, NY 10011;
(800) 354-967

A CIP catalogue record for this book is available from the British Library

ISBN 1 84038 195 7

Publisher: Joanna Lorenz
Editorial Manager: Helen Sudell
Jacket Designer: Nigel Partridge
Designer: Bet Ayer
Photographers: John Freeman, Michelle Garrett, Debbie Patterson
Production Controller: Nick R. Thompson
Reader: Joy Wotton

Previously published as part of a larger compendium, *The Ultimate Rose Book*

The publishers would like to thank the following for designing the arrangements in this
book: Fiona Barnett, Gilly Love, Terence Moore, Katherine Richmond

Printed in Singapore by Star Standard Industries Pte. Ltd.

1 3 5 7 9 10 8 6 4 2

CONTENTS

INTRODUCTION   6

TECHNIQUES

   CARE AND CONDITIONING OF CUT ROSES   8

   DRYING AND STEAMING ROSES   10

   EQUIPMENT AND CONTAINERS   12

   WIRING AND TYING STEMS   14

  ROSE ARRANGEMENTS   16

  INDEX   96

INTRODUCTION

Roses are incredibly versatile and can be used to decorate your home in a variety of ways from table arrangements and baskets to garlands and swags. Along with stunning floral displays, the essential techniques are described, helping you to create beautiful arrangements that will enhance any room in the house.

CARE AND CONDITIONING OF CUT ROSES

Whether you are buying roses or cutting them from the garden, always choose those in the very best condition. Reputable florists, supermarkets and flower stalls take pride in their flowers, selling only good-quality blooms and having the knowledge and experience to keep them that way.

If you are cutting roses from the garden, it is best to do this first thing in the morning, when their water content is highest. Cut the flowers at a sharp angle just above a leaf node and be sure not to be so greedy that you rob each bush of all its blooms or destroy its overall appearance! Place the flowers immediately in a bucket of water, where they can have a long drink before you arrange them.

If you are buying roses, make sure they are well wrapped to avoid excess evaporation and to protect their delicate petals. For long journeys it is better to put them in a bucket of water but, if this is impractical, ask the retailer to cover the stem ends with damp paper. As soon as you reach home, give the flowers a long drink in deep tepid water.

Before arranging the flowers, always cut off any foliage that will fall below the water line in the container or vase. Make a long, diagonal cut from the bottom of each stem, as this will provide the maximum area for water intake. Rose stems should never be crushed with a hammer as so many books advocate. Independent research has proved that this method

ABOVE: *As a gift, lay a bunch of roses and foliage diagonally on a square of paper and fold around the stems. Tie securely with raffia or ribbon.*

destroys the delicate plant cells and makes the stalk less efficient in taking up water; it also encourages the spread of bacterial infection.

Bacteria block the stems and cause the drooping heads so often experienced with shop-bought roses. You can avoid this problem by always using scrupulously clean vases, removing all leaves below the water level and adding commercially formulated flower food. This simple powder contains the correct amount of a mild and completely harmless disinfectant, which inhibits bacterial growth, together with a sugar that

feeds the roses and encourages the flowers to mature and open. If flower food is added to the water it is unnecessary to change it, but it may need topping up in warm weather. Although many people have their own recipes for increasing roses' longevity – lemonade, aspirins, household bleach and so on – flower food is by far the most successful way of keeping roses at their best for longer.

For arrangements using plastic foam, make holes for the rose and other stems with a wooden skewer. If you push the rose stem straight into the foam, particles of foam may become lodged in the base of the stem and prevent good water uptake, causing premature wilting.

If rose heads have wilted, and this may be a result of bacterial infection or an airlock somewhere in the stem, it may be possible to revive them by wrapping them in strong paper and standing the stems in tepid water up to their heads for several hours after first cutting at least 5 cm (2 in) from the end of each stem. If this treatment fails, even more drastic action will be needed and the roses will have to be cut very short in order to perk up their drooping heads.

Finally, there are many theories about rose thorns. Again, research has proved that bacteria may invade the gashes left in the stem when thorns are cut off, so it is better to do this only if the roses are being carried in a bouquet or posy where thorns could prick the hands.

1 Always place roses in a bucket of tepid water for a couple of hours after purchase or cutting.

4 If thorns have to be removed because the roses are being used in a bouquet, use sharp scissors to cut them off, but not too close to the stem.

2 After choosing the vase, cut off any leaves that will fall below the water level, as these will rot and stagnate the water.

5 Add a proprietary flower food to the water in the vase to prolong the life of cut flowers and help to keep the vase water clear.

7 Give first aid to wilting flower heads by wrapping them securely in stiff paper and standing them in a large container of tepid water for a few hours.

3 Using a very sharp knife or pair of scissors, cut the stem diagonally to ensure maximum water uptake.

6 It is sometimes possible to revive wilted roses by cutting the stems very short.

DRYING AND STEAMING ROSES

DRYING ROSES

Roses have been dried for as long as they have been cultivated; their petals have been used in potpourri or the whole stems in decorative arrangements when the fresh flowers were scarce. The Elizabethans preserved roses by immersing them completely in dry sand and keeping them warm until all the moisture had been drawn out. In Victorian times, when houses were heated with open coal fires, which shortened the lives of fresh blooms, intricate dried arrangements were painstakingly created and then covered in glass domes to keep them

dust-free. These rather tortured, contrived designs have long since lost their appeal in preference for looser, more natural arrangements and contemporary designs using dried flowers have gained a new popularity.

There are three principal ways of drying roses: in the air, in a microwave oven and using a desiccant. The latest commercial method is freeze-drying. This successful technique was originally developed as a means to store penicillin and blood plasma during the Second World War. It requires specialized freezers so it is no use putting a bunch of roses in a domestic model. The process can

take up to two weeks and is therefore very expensive but the results are stunning, producing dried roses with all their former intensity of colour and, in some cases, even preserving their perfume. Flowers or bouquets dried by this method can allegedly last for about five years before they start to fade or disintegrate.

Air-drying is the most common method and by far the cheapest as it requires no more than the cost of the roses. This method is best for rosebuds that are just about to open but

BELOW: The easiest way to dry roses is to hang them upside-down in a dark, warm and well ventilated room.

ABOVE: *Once the roses are completely dry, carefully strip off the leaves and tie the buds tightly together. Combined with a halo of dried lavender, a small posy in a terracotta pot makes a delightful gift.*

still have their bud shape. They need to be hung somewhere warm, dry and dark with good ventilation for a couple of weeks – a large airing-cupboard may be ideal. Stringing them together washing-line-style speeds up the process and prevents any moisture being trapped between the flowers, which may develop into mildew. Once they are completely dry, handle them with care as the stems are very brittle. A tight bunch of rose-buds packed together in a small terracotta pot will give added impact to the now-faded colour of the petals. A gentle blow on the lowest setting of a hair drier usually removes most of any dust.

As the flowers need to fit the radius of the turntable, microwave-drying is suitable only for arrange-ments requiring quite short stems. Lay the flowers on greaseproof paper and put into the microwave oven on the lowest setting. The roses need to be checked every minute to prevent "over-cooking".

DESICCANT-DRYING

Desiccant-drying using silica gel crystals or fine sand may be used for fully open roses.

Silica gel is available from some larger pharmacies.

1 Put 1 cm (½ in) of the crystals or sand in an airtight container and lay the rose-heads face up.

2 Cover very carefully with more sifted desiccant until every part of the flower is concealed. Then tightly seal the container and keep at room temperature for approximately seven to ten days before removing from the desiccant.

STEAMING ROSES

This simple technique can greatly improve the appearance of dried roses which are imported in large boxes with up to 25 bunches per box. Frequently, some or all of the bunches arrive at their destination rather squashed. This process will give them a new lease of life, but take care. Never try to open the very centre of the rose, which is often discoloured. The process also works very well for peonies.

2 Remove the rose from the steam and gently push back the outer petals, one by one. Do not tug at the petals or you will find them coming away in your hand.

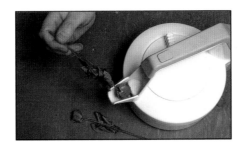

1 Bring a kettle to the boil. Hold the rose by its stem, head down-wards, in the steam for a few seconds, until the outside petals start to waver.

3 If necessary, repeat the steaming process and continue to open the petals, working from the outside towards the centre.

EQUIPMENT AND CONTAINERS

EQUIPMENT

Cellophane · This is useful as a wrapping for a bouquet, as a water-proof lining for containers and scrunched up in a vase of water to support flower stems.

Florist's Adhesive · This sticky glue can be used to attach synthetic and delicate materials which would not withstand the heat of a glue gun.

Florist's Adhesive Tape · This tape is used to secure foam in containers.

Florist's Plastic Foam · Plastic foam comes in a range of shapes and densities, and is available for dry and fresh flowers. Do not re-soak foam used for fresh flowers once it has dried out.

Florist's Scissors · You need a strong, sharp pair of scissors which must be sturdy enough to cut woody stems and even wires.

Florist's Tape · This tape is not adhesive, but the heat of your hands will help secure it to itself. The tape is used to conceal wires and seal stem ends to give an attractive finish.

Florist's Wire · Wire is used to support, control and secure materials, and to extend, strengthen or replace stems. It is available in pre-cut lengths or on a reel. Always use the lightest gauge of wire you can. One of the most useful gauges when working with roses is .71mm (22g).

Glue Gun · The glue gun is electrically powered and fed by sticks of glue, which it melts. It is invaluable in allowing the arranger to attach dried or fresh materials to swags, garlands or circlets securely, cleanly and efficiently. Take care at all times when using a glue gun. Never leave a hot glue gun unattended and avoid using on delicate materials.

Paper Ribbon · This comes in a large range of soft colours. Cut the length required in its twisted state and carefully untwist and flatten it before creating your bows.

Raffia · A natural alternative to string and ribbon, raffia can be used to tie a hand-arranged, spiralled bunch, or to attach bunches to garlands and swags.

Rose Stripper · Squeeze the metal claws together and pull the stripper along the stem to remove thorns and leaves. There is also a blade attachment, to cut stem ends at an angle.

Satin Ribbon · Satin is preferable to synthetic because it is so much softer.

Secateurs · These are necessary to cut the tougher, thicker stems.

String · String is essential when tying spiralled bunches, making garlands or attaching foliage to gates and posts.

Wire Mesh · Plastic foam offers more flexibility but wire mesh is useful. In creating large displays, wire mesh strengthens the foam and prevents it from crumbling. The mesh should be laid over the top of the foam, wrapped around the sides and wedged between it and the container, then secured in place with florist's adhesive tape.

LEFT: *Start with the basic equipment and add items as your skill develops.*

CONTAINERS

While an enormous range of suitable, practical, purpose-made containers is available to the flower arranger, with a little imagination alternatives will present themselves. An old jug or teapot, a pretty mug, an unusual tin, a jam jar, all offer the arranger interesting opportunities.

For fresh flowers, the container must be watertight or properly lined. Consider the scale and proportion of the container both to the particular flowers you are going to use, and the type of arrangement.

Do not forget the container can be a hidden part of the design, simply there to hold the arrangement, or it can be an integral and important feature in the overall finished arrangement.

Baking Tins · Apart from the usual shapes, star, heart, club, spade and diamond shaped baking tins can be used very effectively.

They are particularly good for massed designs, either of fresh or dried flowers, but remember, the tin may need lining.

Baskets · Baskets are an obvious choice for country-style displays. However, there is a wide range of designs to suit many different styles.

Wire or metal baskets are ornate alternatives to wicker and twig, and have a more modern look. Most baskets will need a waterproof lining.

Cast-iron Urns · Though expensive and heavy, cast-iron urns are attractive and will underpin either a large and flowing or contemporary and linear arrangement.

ABOVE: *A varied selection from the vast range of containers that can be used for flower arranging.*

Enamelled Containers · Containers in strong primary colours work well with similarly brightly coloured flowers to produce vibrant displays.

Galvanized Metal Buckets and Pots · These will not rust and their texture is ideal for contemporary displays of both fresh and dried flowers. Lots of shapes and sizes are available but even an old-fashioned bucket can be used.

Glass Vases · The obvious choice, in a wide range; clear glass allows the arrangement to speak for itself. Keep the water scrupulously clean. Frosted, coloured, textured and cut glass all have their place.

Pitchers · Pitchers are ideal receptacles, whether ceramic, glass, enamelled or galvanized metal; short, tall, thin or fat. Displays can range from the rustic and informal to the grand and extravagant.

Pre-formed Plastic Foam Shapes · Pre-formed plastic foam comes in a wide range of shapes and sizes and "novelty" designs, each with a water-tight backing. Equivalent foam shapes are available for dried flowers.

Terracotta Pots · If the arrangement is built in plastic foam, line the pot with cellophane first. Alternatively just pop a jam jar or bowl into the pot to hold the water.

Terracotta pots can be changed very effectively by rubbing them with coloured chalks, or treating them with gold leaf. Organic materials, such as sour milk, will encourage a surface growth to develop, to "age" pots.

Wooden Trugs and Boxes · Particularly suitable for enhancing country-style designs, rubbing with coloured chalk can create an entirely new look. Remember to line with waterproof material.

WIRING AND TYING STEMS

TAPING STEMS AND WIRES

Stems and wires are covered with florist's tape for three reasons. First, cut materials which have been wired can no longer take up water and covering these with tape seals in the moisture that already exists in the stem. Second, the tape conceals the wires. Third, wired dried materials are covered with florist's tape to ensure that the material does not slip out of the wired mount.

1 Hold the wired stem near its top with the end of a length of florist's tape between the thumb and index finger of your left hand (or the opposite way if you are left-handed). Hold the remainder of the length of tape at 45° to the wired stem, keeping it taut. Starting at the top of the stem, just above the wires, rotate the flower slowly, to wrap the tape around both the stem and wires, working down.

2 While taping the wired stem you may wish to add further stems, setting the flower-heads at different heights as you tape, to create "units". Finally, fasten off just above the end of the wires, by squeezing the tape against itself to stick it securely.

MAKING A STAY WIRE

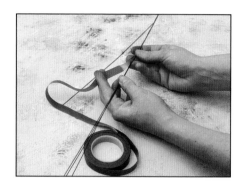

1 Group together four florist's wires, each overlapping the next by about 3 cm (1¼ in). Start taping the wires together from one end.

2 As the tape reaches the end of the first wire add another wire to the remaining three ends of wires and continue taping, and so on, adding wires and taping four together until you achieve the required length.

SINGLE LEG MOUNT

This is for wiring flowers which have a strong natural stem or where a double weight of wire is not necessary.

1 Hold the flowers or foliage between your thumb and index finger, while taking the weight of the material across the top of your hand. Position a wire behind the stem one-third up from the bottom.

2 Bend the wire ends together with one leg shorter than the other. Holding the short wire leg parallel with the stem, wrap the long wire leg around both the stem and the other wire leg. Straighten the long wire.

DOUBLE-LEG MOUNT

This is formed in the same way as the single-leg mount but extends the stem with two equal-length wire legs.

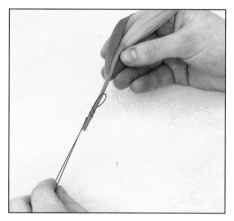

1 Hold the flower or foliage between the thumb and index finger of your left hand (or opposite way if you are left-handed) while taking the weight of the plant material across the top of your hand. Position a wire and length behind the stem about one-third of the way up from the bottom. One-third of the wire should be to one side of the stem. Bend the wire parallel to the stem. One leg will be about twice as long as the other.

2 Holding the shorter leg against the stem, wrap the longer leg around both stem and the other wire to secure. Straighten both legs which should now be of equal length.

WIRING A ROSE-HEAD

Roses have relatively thick, woody stems so, to make them suitable for use in intricate work the natural stem needs to be replaced with a wire stem.

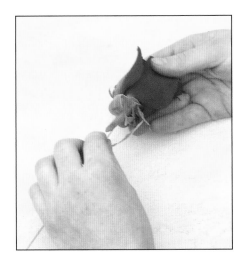

1 Cut the stem of the rose to a length of about 3 cm (1¼ in). Push one end of a florist's wire through the seed-box of the rose at the side. Holding the head of the rose in your left hand (opposite way if you are left-handed), wrap the wire firmly around and down the stem.

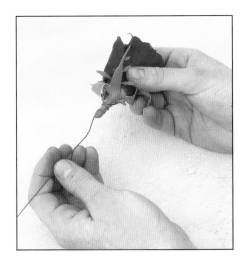

2 Straighten the remaining wire to extend the natural stem. Cover the wire and stem with florist's tape.

TYING POSIES

Simple, hand-tied posies are a very special gift and their diminutive size implies an intimacy that makes them personal and unique. The smaller the posy, the tinier and more delicate the flowers and foliage need to be. Wispy, frond-like leaves define the shape of individual flower-heads, particularly if the colours are similar, and this will give the posy more clarity.

1 Put the roses in a spiralling bunch and surround with rose leaves. Bind the flowers with raffia and trim the stems. Leaving enough ribbon to tie a bow, start winding the ribbon from the top, overlapping each twist to conceal the raffia and the stems.

2 When you reach the bottom, tuck the ribbon over the base of the stems and then wind the ribbon back up the stems.

3 When you reach the starting point, tie the ribbon in a knot before adding a bow and cut the ribbon ends on a slant to help to prevent any fraying.

FRESH VALENTINE TERRACOTTA POTS

With luck, Valentine's Day brings with it red roses, but these small jewel-like arrangements present them in an altogether different way. The deep red of the roses visually links the two pots: contrasting with the acid lime green of 'Santini' chrysanthemums in one, and combining richly with purple phlox in the other.

MATERIALS
half block plastic foam
2 small terracotta pots, 1 slightly
    larger than the other
cellophane
knife
scissors
ming fern
ivy leaves

5 stems 'Santini' spray
    chrysanthemums
6 stems purple phlox
18 stems dark red roses

1 Soak the plastic foam in water. Line both the terracotta pots with cellophane. Cut the foam into small blocks and wedge them into the lined pots. Trim the cellophane to fit. Do not trim too close to the edge of the pot.

2 Build a dome-shaped foliage outline in proportion to each pot, using ming fern in the larger pot and ivy leaves in the smaller one.

3 In the larger pot, arrange 'Santini' chrysanthemums amongst the ming fern. In the small pot, distribute the phlox amongst the ivy.

4 Strip the leaves and thorns from the roses, cut the stems to length and arrange in both displays.

ABOVE LEFT: Arrange roses together or singly.

SMALL FRESH ROSE VALENTINE'S RING

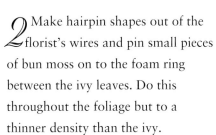

2 Make hairpin shapes out of the florist's wires and pin small pieces of bun moss on to the foam ring between the ivy leaves. Do this throughout the foliage but to a thinner density than the ivy.

3 Cut the leaves and thorns off the roses. Cut the rose stems to approximately 3.5 cm (1⅜ in) long and push them into the foam until the ring is evenly covered. The ivy leaves should still be visible in between the rose-heads.

*W*hile this delightful floral circlet could be used at any time of the year, the impact created by the massed red roses makes it particularly appropriate to Valentine's Day. It can be hung on a wall or, with a candle at its centre, used as a table decoration for a romantic dinner for two.

MATERIALS

15 cm (6 in) diameter plastic foam ring
dark green ivy leaves
florist's wires
bun moss
20 stems dark red roses
scissors

1 Soak the plastic foam ring in water. Push individual, medium-sized ivy leaves into the foam, to create an even foliage outline all around the ring.

ABOVE LEFT: If you receive a Valentine's Day bouquet of red roses, why not recycle them? After the rose blooms have fully blown open, cut down their stems for use in this circlet, to extend their lives.

ROSE CROWNS FOR ALL SEASONS

Roses can be enjoyed all year round. Garden roses start blooming in mid-spring and continue into late autumn, if the weather is mild. During the barren winter months, there are still hundreds of commercially grown roses to choose from. Just as a garden enjoys a change of season with different colours, shapes and scents, you can acknowledge the shifting calendar inside your home. It is a practical investment to acquire a versatile container – perhaps an old china soup tureen or vase – that gives scope to a range of decorative ideas. It should be large enough to hold several small vases and candles, and also be deep enough to be used as a planter.

SPRING

The darker pink and red freesias used in this arrangement have a strong scent. Paler pink tulips present a contrast in shape to the 'Louise Odier' rose, a camellia-like Bourbon rose which flowers almost continuously through the summer. The lacy foliage of bupleurum has the same delicate qualities as *Alchemilla mollis*, another good filler for later in the year.

SUMMER

Sunflowers radiate bright vitality and are synonymous with hot summer days. The smaller-headed varieties are more practical for arrangements, as those with heads the size of dinner plates are too heavy and dominating and are best left to grow in the

SPRING

SUMMER

AUTUMN

WINTER

garden. 'Tina' is one of the commercially grown larger-flowered spray roses; it has a rich buttery colour and a slight scent.

AUTUMN

Rosa pimpinellifolia or 'Scotch Briar' is an ancient hardy rose which produces creamy-white single flowers and, later, almost black hips. The latter are combined here with dusty pink mop-heads of hydrangea and a stunning commercially grown rose called 'Baccarole'. Its red wine-coloured petals develop a faint but obvious perfume.

WINTER

Create an elegant centrepiece for a Christmas table with white and cream roses, varying shades of green foliage and non-drip candles. Several very late flowering 'Boule de Neige' Bourbon roses are supplemented with the commercially grown 'White Success'. Grey-green eucalyptus blends with symphoricarpos (snowberry) and trailing variegated ivy.

ABOVE: *A crown-shaped container is packed with an assortment of different shapes and sizes of jars and bottles.*

WARNING: Never leave candles burning unattended.

OLD-FASHIONED GARDEN ROSE ARRANGEMENT

LEFT: *The technique is to mass several varieties of rose, whose papery petals will achieve a textural mix of colour and scent.*

2 Position the longer-stemmed blooms in the pitcher with the heads massed tightly together. This ensures that the cut stems are supported and so can simply be placed directly in the water.

3 Mass shorter, more open flower-heads in the container inside the plant pot with the stems hidden and the heads showing just above the rim of the pot. The heads look best if kept either all on one level or in a slight dome shape. If fewer flowers are used, wire mesh or plastic foam may be needed to control the positions of individual blooms.

*T*he beautiful full-blown blooms of these antique-looking roses give an opulent and romantic feel to a very simple combination of flower and container. This arrangement deserves centre stage in any room setting.

MATERIALS
*watertight container, to put inside
    plant pot
squat weathered terracotta pot
pitcher
short- and long-stemmed garden roses
scissors*

1 Place the watertight container inside the terracotta pot and fill with water. Fill the pitcher as well. Select and prepare your blooms and remove the lower foliage and thorns.

RUBY WEDDING DISPLAY

*F*ormal looking, but simple in construction, this Ruby Wedding arrangement is a lavish mass of deep purple tulips and velvety red roses set against the dark glossy green of camellia leaves. A beautiful paper bow completes the effect.

MATERIALS
bowl
10 short stems camellia foliage
scissors
20 red roses
10 purple tulips
paper ribbon

ABOVE: *Designed as a table arrangement complete with celebratory bow around its container, this display of rich and passionate colours would be a magnificent gift.*

1 Approximately three-quarters fill the bowl with water. Remove the lower foliage from the camellia stems and roses and remove the thorns. Cut the stems of camellia and roses to 7.5 cm (3 in) longer than the depth of the container. Arrange the camellia stems in the bowl, to create a low domed foliage outline, within which the flowers will be arranged. Arrange half the roses evenly throughout the camellia foliage.

2 Cut the tulip stems to approximately 7.5 cm (3 in) longer than the depth of the bowl and strip away any remaining lower leaves from the stems. Position the tulips in the display, distributing them evenly throughout the roses and camellia. Finally, add the remaining roses evenly throughout the arrangement to complete a dense, massed flower effect of deep red hues.

3 Form a festive bow from the paper ribbon. The bow should be substantial but it is important that it is kept in scale with the display. To complete the arrangement, tie the bow to the container so that it sits on the front.

TABLE STYLING WITH ROSES

Even the simplest meal can be transformed into something quite special with the addition of a few beautiful flowers to the table. In summer, when garden roses are plentiful, it takes only a few to add their delicious, delicate scent to a table setting. The strongest perfume comes from those that are in full bloom. Their heavy heads need to be cut short and may need the support of some other foliage, such as lavender or rosemary in a simple arrangement.

Commercially grown roses are usually sold in bud, so buy them a few days before they are needed to ensure that the roses open to produce large clusters of small flower-heads that are perfect for low arrangements. Floral designs for tables are best kept short, so diners can see across the table and plates can be passed without any obstacles. Alternatively, tall candelabra can be decorated with delicate foliage, with rose-heads wired to the candle holders. A piece of plastic foam fitted around the base of each candle can be concealed with foliage and short stems of roses gently pushed into it.

For special parties, a rose tucked inside a napkin ring for each guest is a personal welcome. Co-ordinating the colour of the flowers with the food and table linen looks stylish and professional. A table centre of floating candles and roses is a simple idea for dinner parties and can be particularly attractive if both roses and candles

OPPOSITE: *'Felicia' is one of the finest of the hybrid musk roses and three or four blooms arranged with a few sprigs of rosemary in a small glass inside a terracotta pot make a natural tablesetting. Commercially grown 'Baccarole' roses take several days to open fully and their blue-crimson colour needs only a few campanula leaves to create a rich, luxurious decoration for the table.*

are sweetly scented. According to the Ancient Romans, the addition of some fragrant rose petals to the wine delayed the intoxication of its drinkers! A bottle of sparkling white or rosé wine and then sprinkled with petals makes a delightful way of serving this drink – or make rose petal punch by adding sugar, rose petals and raspberry liqueur to the wine.

ABOVE: *'Brown Velvet' is a modern cluster-flowered rose. Just a couple of stems are needed to fill a small vase, and its dark brown-red colour makes an ideal accompaniment to a plate of strawberries.*

ROSES IN DIFFERENT CONTAINERS

Virtually anything can be used to hold roses, from a simple jam jar to the most expensive crystal vase. What is more important is its shape – do avoid those types of vases with tight little necks that can take only a few stems, forcing them into an uncomfortable position. Allow the roses to be the centre of attention and increase their longevity by following the instructions for conditioning roses earlier in the book.

ABOVE LEFT: *A shallow glass bowl holding a couple of floating rose-heads makes an effective small decoration for a bedside table or similar surface that is viewed from above. Shown here is the sweetly fragrant garden rose 'Iris Webb'.*

ABOVE: *A few stems of roses make a stronger statement when held together with a piece of garden raffia. This rose is the commercially grown 'Prelude' with eucalyptus stems.*

LEFT: *If you regularly cut roses from the garden, a wide, shallow glass dish on a pedestal is a good choice for the irregularly shaped stems, particularly of old roses. Here is the garden rose 'Felicia'.*

ABOVE: *The price of commercially grown roses is often determined by the stem length. Their elegant straight stalks may be more than 60 cm (24 in) long. This beautiful rose is commercially grown 'Konfetti'.*

BELOW: *Increase the impact of the blooms by grouping them in tumblers of contrasting colours. The roses, left to right, are: 'Julia's Rose', 'Edith Holden', 'Iced Ginger', 'Peppermint Ice'; front: 'Josephine Bruce'.*

ABOVE: *A few sprays of a fragrant rose are all that are needed to impart scent to a small room or hallway. The picture shows the garden rose 'Amber Queen'. Cut roses from a bush carefully, so as not to destroy the overall shape or strip it bare, choosing blooms that would otherwise be concealed from view.*

TIED POSY

Flowers are at their most appealing when kept simple. Just gather together some garden cuttings and arrange them in a pretty posy that the recipient can simply unwrap and put straight into a vase, without further ado.

MATERIALS

secateurs

3 stems roses

10-12 stems eucalyptus

3 stems scabious

brown paper

ribbon

1 Using sharp secateurs, carefully cut each flower stem to approximately 15 cm (6 in) long. Remove the lower leaves and trim any thorns from the roses.

2 Gather the flowers together, surrounding each rose with some feathery eucalyptus, and then adding the scabious.

ABOVE: *"Cottage-garden" flowers, such as roses and scabious, are elegantly set against the cool green eucalyptus in this deceptively simple posy that has masses of impact.*

3 Wrap the posy with paper and secure it with a length of ribbon, tied simply in a pretty bow.

SUMMER GIFT BASKET

Fresh roses are always a welcome gift – make them into something extra special by laying them in a basket with prettily packaged, home-made strawberry jam.

MATERIALS

jar of strawberry jam
pink paper
glue
paper strawberry print
scissors
glazed pink paper
raffia
wooden basket
coloured paper
roses

1 Make up a pretty presentation for the strawberry jam by wrapping the jar with pink paper and gluing on a paper strawberry print, to fix the paper.

2 Make a top of glazed pink paper and a raffia tie. Line the basket with coloured paper and fill it with a bunch of roses, tied with raffia, and the strawberry jam.

ABOVE: *Combining a gift of roses and home-made jam in a pretty wooden basket, with toning colours of flowers, paper and jam, makes the gift seem much more special than just giving them separately.*

MOTHER'S DAY BASKET

What could be a more delightful surprise for a mother on her special day than a basket of roses and lilies, arranged with style and sent with love? The basket, painted to tone with the flowers, becomes a permanent keepsake. It would be ideal to hold wools, sewing materials, or bath preparations.

MATERIALS

shallow basket with handle
block plastic foam
waterproof liner, such as plastic box
narrow florist's adhesive tape
scissors
long-lasting foliage, such as
  eucalyptus
several stems flowering shrub
about 12 stems pink and cream roses
about 12 stems alstroemeria
  (Peruvian lilies)
secateurs
paper ribbon
florist's wire

1 As the basket is so much part of the gift, choose a decorative one with care. The basket illustrated, with woven, twisted cane, was painted in uneven stripes of pink gloss paint, to add a touch of sparkle to the overall arrangement. This colour is repeated in the floral-printed paper ribbon bow, a flamboyant finishing touch to the design.

2 Soak the plastic foam well. Put the liner in the basket and place the block of foam in it. Cut two strips of adhesive tape and criss-cross them over the foam and down on to the sides of the basket, to hold the foam firmly in place. Arrange the tallest stems of foliage to make a fan shape at the back of the basket. Cut progressively shorter stems for the centre and front, positioning them so they droop and trail over the rim of the basket.

3 Trim the roses and remove the lower leaves and any thorns. Arrange the roses to make a gently rounded shape, alternating the colours, pink and cream, so that each complements the other.

4 Add the alstroemeria, cutting some individual flowers on short stems and positioning them close against the foam. Fill in the gaps with short sprays of flowering shrub.

5 Unfurl the twisted ribbon by pulling it out from one end.

6 Cut the length of ribbon required and tie it into a bow. Trim the ribbon ends. Thread the florist's wire through the back of the knot, twist and insert the two ends into the foam at the front of the basket. Mist the flowers with cool water, and keep the foam moist before you deliver it.

OPPOSITE: *A basket arrangement is a wonderful way to give expensive roses maximum impact.*

A DOZEN ROSES

The romantic tradition of giving a dozen red roses is all too often confined to Valentine's Day, when worldwide demand for red roses is so great that they become outrageously expensive. However, since roses are available all year round, why not use the idea of styling with a dozen roses for other times of the year?

Commercial rose breeders have at last recognized the universal desire for perfumed flowers and are producing exceptional roses that are scented. 'Prelude' is a beautiful dark lilac-coloured rose that has a soft sweet perfume which increases as the blooms open and can last for more than ten days.

ABOVE: Combine the roses with complementary flowers such as darker pink arum lilies and lilac pink alstroemeria (Peruvian lilies).

TOP: Cut the roses quite short and arrange in a bowl filled with a close-fitting piece of well-soaked florist's foam. Add pieces of foliage to create a rounded shape.

LEFT: Cut the roses to different lengths and mix with other materials in different containers.

1 Arrange the long-stemmed roses simply in a tall glass vase.

2 Buy or pick fresh green foliage to increase the size of your arrangement.

3 Using a rustic twig circle, tie small pieces of well-soaked florist's foam at intervals and cover them with foliage or moss. Carefully make small holes with a sharp stick in each piece. Place the roses in groups of two or three and keep the foam moist.

4 Make a table centrepiece of the roses in a basket with candles.

5 Line a large basket with polythene (plastic) and fill with small compatible houseplants, leaving space for one or more vases to hold the roses. Cover the surface with moss, to conceal the tops of the vases.

6 Before the roses open, hang them upside-down to air-dry.

7 Once the roses have opened but before they start to "blow", place them in a large shallow container of sand and allow to dry.

RIGHT: Tie the roses into a pompom shape, using a piece of string or garden raffia, and place in a narrow glass vase or jam jar that is tall enough to support them. Stand this in a flower pot or planter and cover the top with moss, to create the effect of a tree. Keep well topped up with water.

TABLE ARRANGEMENT WITH FRUIT AND FLOWERS

The addition of fruit brings a visual opulence to this arrangement of flowers. The sumptuous reds and purples of the figs and grapes used in this display harmonize beautifully with the rich, deep hues of the flowers. The natural bloom on the fruit combines with the velvet softness of the roses to create a textural feast for the eye. The overall effect is one of ravishing lusciousness.

MATERIALS
basket
cellophane
2 blocks plastic foam
scissors
florist's adhesive tape
1 bundle tree ivy
3 bunches red grapes
florist's wires
6 black figs
15 stems antirrhinum
15 stems amaranthus (straight, not trailing)
15 stems astilbe
20 stems red roses
5 stems hydrangea

ABOVE: *Make sure that all your chosen material enhances the colour of the roses.*

1 Line the basket with cellophane and tightly wedge in the blocks of water-soaked plastic foam. Trim the excess cellophane around the edge of the basket. If the arrangement is to be moved, tape the foam firmly in place.

2 To establish the overall shape of the arrangement, create a low dome of foliage with the tree ivy in proportion with the size and shape of the basket. Spread the tree ivy evenly throughout the plastic foam.

3 Wire the bunches of grapes by double-leg mounting on florist's wires. Position the bunches recessed in the foliage in a roughly diagonal line across the display. Handle the grapes delicately.

4 Push a wire through each fig from side to side, leaving projecting ends to bend downwards. Group the figs in pairs and push the wires into the plastic foam around the centre of the arrangement.

ABOVE: Although there are many ingredients in this display, the spectacular final effect is well worth the extra attention.

5 Emphasize the domed shape of the display with the antirrhinums, amaranthus and astilbe. Remove lower foliage and thorns from the roses, which are the focal flowers, and add them evenly through the display. To complete the arrangement, recess the hydrangea heads into the plastic foam, to give depth and texture. Water the foam daily to prolong the life of the display.

OLD-FASHIONED GARDEN ROSE POSY

This tiny hand-tied posy of blown red and pale apricot roses and mint is designed to accompany a circlet headdress for a young bridesmaid. The velvet beauty of the contents gives it charm and impact.

MATERIALS

5 stems deep red and 5 stems pale
apricot roses
scissors
20 stems mint
6 vine leaves
string
raffia

1 Remove all thorns and lower leaves from the rose stems. Starting with a rose in one hand, add alternately two stems of mint and one rose stem until all the materials are used. Keep turning the posy as you build, to form the stems into a spiral. Finally, add the vine leaves to form an edging to the arrangement and tie with string at the binding point (where the stems cross).

ABOVE: *Finished with a natural raffia bow, the posy has a fresh, just-gathered look. Happily, it is very simple to make.*

2 Trim the ends of the stems so that they are approximately one-third of the overall height of the posy. Tie raffia around the binding point.

TOPIARY ROSE TREE

This simple little double-headed tree makes a change from conventional arrangements. 'Yellow Dot' commercially grown spray roses open fully to a pretty rosette shape. The same design could be made up using dried rose-buds but you would need considerably more flowers and you would need to use plastic foam for dried flowers. Kept cool and frequently misted, this fresh rose tree should last for at least a week.

MATERIALS
2 spheres and 1 rectangular block
  plastic foam
knife
sturdy terracotta pot
3 bamboo canes
thick pliable string
secateurs
10 stems leucadendron
10 stems spray roses
sphagnum moss

1 *(Below left)* Soak the foam. Cut a piece of the rectangular block to fit in the pot. Insert the canes together and position the foam spheres on the canes. Bind the string around the canes.

2 *(Below right)* Cut off the leucadendron heads, leaving about 2 cm (¾ in) of stem, and insert into the foam spheres at regular intervals. Insert the roses in the same way. Cover the surface of the foam in the pot with sphagnum moss.

ABOVE: *For an effective rose tree select roses that open fully to provide a rosette shape. Remember to leave enough space around each rose for the bloom to open without being squashed.*

ROSE AND FRUIT BASKET

For a special dinner party or to decorate a side food table, this ornate moss-covered basket could contain either commercially grown or garden roses. Whichever roses you choose, it is important to select a sympathetically coloured fruit or berry to enhance the flowers. 'Prelude' is a commercially grown scented rose and its lilac tone is co-ordinated here with branches of small, immature purple plums and darker elderberry fronds. Crimson rose-hips and crab apples would look stunning with red, orange or yellow roses but for roses with a cream and white colouring, green fruits or vegetables, such as greengages and baby artichokes, would create a more effective result.

Dried poppy heads make a good contrast in shape to the roses.

MATERIALS

block plastic foam
knife
plastic bowl
string
sphagnum moss
wire basket
several small branches small plums
    and elderberry fruits
6 poppy seed-heads
8 stems roses
3 beeswax candles

WARNING: Never leave candles burning unattended.

BELOW: Rose-heads are less fragile and easier to manipulate when they are in bud, but allow enough room in the display for the blooms to open without disrupting the other elements.

1 Cut the foam to fit snugly in the bowl. Soak the foam in water until it is completely saturated. Wedge into the bowl and secure with string if the fit is not tight. Arrange the moss around the bowl to conceal it within the basket.

2 Make the initial shape of the arrangement using just the foliage and poppy heads.

3 Remove the lower foliage and thorns from the roses. Place the roses randomly, turning the basket to see the effect from all sides. Avoid putting the roses too close together. Then place the candles securely, making sure that no foliage or flowers will be near the flames.

ROSE AND HERB BASKET

Fresh flowers and herbs make a perfect partnership. The scent of the roses and herbs together is subtle but wonderful, especially if you hang the arrangement where you will brush lightly against it as you pass – but do not place it so that the roses are in danger of being crushed. If you do not have the herbs listed here, there are many alternatives, such as sage and rosemary and the leaves of any evergreen shrub.

MATERIALS
1 block plastic foam
small flower basket, with handle
plastic sheet
florist's adhesive tape
scissors
hellebore leaves
scented geranium leaves
12 small sprays golden oregano
12 stems cream roses

1 Soak the foam well. Line the basket with the plastic sheet, so that no water will seep through the basketwork. Put the foam block inside the liner and hold it in with tape. Cover the foam completely with a mixture of hellebore leaves and scented geranium leaves.

2 Add the sprays of golden oregano, placing them so that there will be room between them for the roses. Remove the lower foliage

and any thorns from the roses. Place the roses evenly throughout the arrangement, putting six on each side of the handle so that the arrangement looks well balanced, but not too symmetrical. Top up the foam with water each day to prolong the life of the arrangement.

BELOW: A delightful country-style arrangement of roses and herbs brings the mingled scents of a summer garden into the house.

APRICOT ROSES AND PUMPKINS

The simple appeal of this design results from its use of just one type of flower and one type of foliage. The addition of tiny pumpkins gives body to the pretty combination of spray roses and flowering hypericum foliage. Note how the apricot colour is carried through flowers, pumpkins and container, complemented by the red buds and the yellow flowers of the hypericum.

MATERIALS
1 block plastic foam
knife
marble bird bath or similar container
florist's adhesive tape
scissors
10 stems hypericum
5 tiny pumpkins
florist's wires
10 stems apricot spray roses

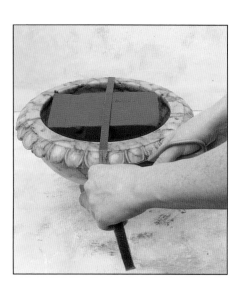

1 Soak the block of plastic foam and cut it so that it can be wedged in place in the container. Secure the foam with florist's adhesive tape.

2 Create the outline of the display using the hypericum, and establish its overall height, width and length. The stems of commercially produced hypericum tend to be long and straight, with many offshoots of smaller stems. To create a more delicate foliage effect, and to get the most out of your material, use these smaller stems in the arrangement.

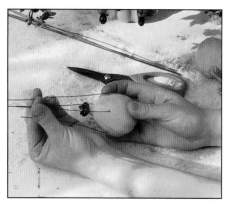

3 Wire each pumpkin by pushing one wire right through across the pumpkin base and out of the other side. Push another wire through to cross the first at right angles. Pull both wires down so that they project from the base. The pumpkins will be supported by pushing these wires into the plastic foam.

4 Position the pumpkins in the foliage, making sure that some are recessed more than others.

5 Remove any thorns and the lower foliage from the roses. Infill the arrangement with the spray roses. Like the hypericum, spray roses tend to have lots of small offshoots from the main stem and these should be used to get the most out of your materials. To augment the overall shape of the display, use buds on longer stems at the outside edges, with the most open blooms and heavily flowered stems in the centre.

OPPOSITE: *Substituting limes for the pumpkins will add a touch of vibrancy; for a more sophisticated look, use plums or black grapes.*

MINIATURE ROSES

A long-lasting gift for rose-lovers is *Rosa chinensis*, the pygmy or China rose. Modern miniature varieties of this species are available in flower all year round, and make a delightful alternative to cut flowers.

MATERIALS
wooden basket
plastic sheet
scissors
florist's adhesive tape
crocks
compost
3 miniature rose plants
sphagnum moss

1 Line the basket with a plastic sheet, securing it with florist's adhesive tape.

2 Arrange crocks over the base of the basket. Fill with compost.

3 Remove the rose plants from their pots and arrange them in the basket.

ABOVE: *Another idea is to make a fragrant* pot à fleurs, *using a basket that will hold a couple of miniature roses and a foliage plant.*

4 Pack moss into any spaces and cover the soil.

ABOVE: Other flowers and foliage that combine well with these tiny rose-heads need to be of a similar proportion, such as narcissi, lily of the valley, lavender, Nepeta mussinii, campanula or viola plants.

LEFT: Miniature roses planted in a long basket interspersed with herbs such as oregano, thyme or bush basil make an inside window-box for a kitchen or bathroom.

CELEBRATION TABLE DECORATION

A table for any celebratory lunch will not usually have much room to spare on it. In this instance there is no room for the wine cooler, and the answer is to incorporate this large, but necessary piece of catering equipment within the flower arrangement.

The floral decoration is a sumptuous, textural display of gold, yellow and white flowers with green and grey foliage. The spiky surfaces of the chestnuts add a wonderful variation in texture.

MATERIALS

40 cm (15 in) diameter plastic
    foam ring

scissors

25 stems Senecio laxifolius

15 stems elaeagnus

3 groups 2 chestnuts

florist's wires

thick gloves

18 stems yellow roses

10 stems cream-coloured Eustoma
    grandiflorum

10 stems solidago

10 stems flowering fennel

ABOVE: *The arrangement is based on a circular, plastic foam ring with the centre left open to accommodate the wine cooler. The splendid silver wine cooler is enhanced by the beauty of the flowers and, in turn, its highly polished surface reflects the flowers to increase their visual impact. This magnificent arrangement would make a stunning centrepiece for a wedding table.*

1 Soak the plastic foam ring in water. Cut the senecio to around 14 cm (5½ in) and distribute it evenly around the ring, leaving the centre clear.

4 Still wearing your gloves, arrange the groups of chestnuts at three equidistant points around the circumference of the plastic foam ring, and secure them by pushing the wires into the plastic foam.

5 Cut down the rose stems to approximately 14 cm (5½ in), remove lower foliage and any thorns and arrange in staggered groups of three roses at six points around the ring, equal distances apart, pushing the stems firmly into the plastic foam.

2 Cut the elaeagnus to a length of about 14 cm (5½ in) and distribute evenly throughout the senecio to reinforce the foliage outline, still leaving the centre of the plastic foam clear to accommodate the wine cooler.

3 Double-leg mount three groups of two chestnuts on wire and cut the wire legs to about 6 cm (2¼ in). Take care, as the chestnuts are very prickly and it is advisable to wear heavy-duty gardening gloves.

6 Cut stems of eustoma flower-heads 12 cm (4¾ in) long from the main stem. Arrange the stems evenly in the foam. Cut the stems of solidago to a length of about 14 cm (5½ in) and distribute throughout. Finally, cut the stems of fennel to about 12 cm (4¾ in) long and add evenly through the display, pushing the stems into the plastic foam.

VALENTINE'S HEART CIRCLET

ABOVE: *This takes a little more effort than ordering a bunch of flowers from your florist, but that effort will be seen as a measure of your devotion.*

*I*nstead of the traditional dozen red roses, why not give the love of your life a wall-hanging decoration for Valentine's Day?

Set your heart (in this case wooden) in a circlet of dried materials full of romantic associations – red roses to demonstrate your passion, honesty to affirm the truth of your feelings and lavender for the sweetness of your love.

MATERIALS
33 heads dried red roses
scissors
silver reel wire
florist's tape
55 stems dried lavender
10 stems dried honesty
florist's wires
1 small wooden heart, on a string

1 Cut the dried rose stems to approximately 2.5 cm (1 in) and individually double-leg mount on silver reel wires, then cover the stems with tape. Group three rose-heads together and double-leg mount on reel wire. Cover the stems with tape. Repeat the process for all the rose-heads, making in total eleven groups.

Group the dried lavender into bunches of five stems and double-leg mount on silver reel wire, then tape. Repeat the process for all the lavender, making eleven groups.

Cut pods from stems of dried honesty, group into threes and double-leg mount them on silver reel wires and tape. Make eleven groups.

Make a stay wire from florist's wires.

2 Lay a group of the honesty pods over one end of the stay wire and tape on securely. Then add, so that they just overlap, a group of lavender stems followed by a group of rose-heads, taping each group to the stay wire. Keep repeating this sequence, all the while bending the stay wire into a circle.

3 When the circle is complete, cut off any excess stay wire, leaving approximately 3 cm (1¼ in) to overlap. Then tape the two ends together through the dried flowers, to secure. Tie the string from the wooden heart on to the stay wire between the dried blooms, so that the heart hangs in the centre of the circlet.

HEART-SHAPED ROSE WREATH

This striking decoration uses a single type of rose in one colour.

MATERIALS
florist's wires
florist's tape
scissors
50 stems dried red roses
silver reel wire

1 Make a stay wire with florist's wires and tape. Form it into a heart shape about 22 cm (8¾ in) high, with the two ends of the wire meeting at its bottom point.

2 Cut the rose stems to about 2.5 cm (1 in). Double-leg mount them on silver reel wire and tape.

ABOVE: *This effective heart would make an unusual and long-lasting Valentine's Day gift.*

3 Starting at the top, tape the rose stems to the stay wire. Slightly overlap the roses to achieve a continuous line of heads, finishing at its bottom point. Starting back at the top, repeat the process around the other half of the heart. Tape the two ends of the wire together.

DOUBLE-HEART BASKET

This romantic flower basket, made from two interlocking hearts, is an intriguing present. The basic shape is moulded from fine wire mesh and covered in moss, to give it a fresh and natural appearance. One heart is packed with roses and the other piled high with strawberries and currants for a summertime treat – once the fruit has been eaten the basket could be filled with pot-pourri or trinkets.

MATERIALS

wire mesh

pliers

thick gloves

dried sphagnum moss

glue gun

1 block plastic foam for dried flowers

large bunch dried roses

scissors

fresh strawberries and currants

2 Cover the hearts with handfuls of moss, using a glue gun to fix it in place. Press the moss right into the mesh, so that all of the wire is covered without losing the outline.

3 (Right) From the plastic foam, cut a heart shape to fit inside the left-hand heart and stick in place. Snip off the dried rose-heads and push a line of flowers into the edge of the foam.

4 Fill the centre space with more roses, placing them close together to form a cushion-like effect. Just before presentation, fill the second heart with strawberries and currants.

1 Cut a 30 x 60 cm (12 x 24 in) piece of wire mesh. Halfway along, cut about 7.5 cm (3 in) into the wire at both top and bottom. Carefully mould the wire into two hearts, bending the mesh over to form a point at the bottom and two curves at the top. It is a good idea to wear gardening gloves while doing this.

ABOVE: *As an alternative to strawberries and currants, you could fill the second basket with a selection of shells and berries.*

OPPOSITE: *Roses and hearts are natural partners for romantic gifts but in folk-art the heart is a symbol of friendship, making this a gift suitable for any occasion.*

$\mathcal{S}$IMPLE POT OF ROSES

ABOVE: *A simple rose pot display can be made in single colours or, as here, with a combination. Make a matching pair to stand on a mantelpiece or shelf for a symmetrical, formal effect, or perhaps add a fabric bow for a softer, more romantic appearance.*

$\mathcal{Y}$ou do not need to wire the roses into bunches for this large pot. Instead, carefully place them in the foam one at a time, making sure that the rose-heads are well spaced, to create a good balance. You can add one or two other varieties of dried material to the display, if you like, but it will look most effective if the design is kept as simple as possible. When using roses alone in a large display, steam the heads open a little way before you start work. Bought flowers often look squashed and, as they are such an important part of this display, they should look their best. For a really stunning effect, use different combinations of size and colour, and try to retain as much of the green leaf as possible.

MATERIALS
terracotta pot
1 block plastic foam for dried
    flowers
knife
about 30 stems dried roses,
    in various colours
scissors
sphagnum moss
glue gun (optional)
florist's wires (optional)

1 Invert the pot and press to form an indentation on the foam block. Following the line the pot has made, cut off the excess foam with a sharp knife.

2 Trim the foam to fit the pot tightly and push in.

3 Press the foam firmly down into the pot; trim the top so that the foam and the top of the pot are level.

4 Trim each rose stem to the required length as you work. In the finished display, the roses should be at different levels so that the heads do not obscure or crowd each other.

6 Continue to press flowers into the pot; if you are using more than one colour, ensure that you have a good mix of hues over the display.

7 Finally, fix moss around the base of the roses with a glue gun, taking care not to burn yourself on the hot glue. Alternatively, bend short florist's wires over, to form U-shaped staples that can be pushed into the foam to trap the moss.

5 Start in the middle of the foam, pressing in the tallest rose. Then work outwards, continuing to add the stems one by one. Arrange the roses to any height, but make sure that they are a good balance for the size of the pot that you are using.

RIGHT: *The colours of these peachy-pink and yellow roses are naturally offset by the subdued green moss and terracotta. Wherever possible, try to use antique terracotta pots, which have a pleasing texture and sympathetic look. If you can only obtain plastic pots, you can always conceal them in outer containers that reflect the colours of the display.*

ROSE AND POTPOURRI GARLAND

This is a delicate and pretty garland, which uses a hop-vine ring as its base. These are fairly inexpensive and can be purchased ready-made from good florists. If you prefer, you could make your own, using vines or twigs cut when green so that they are pliable. Weave them together to form a ring and leave it to dry completely, when it will hold its shape.

MATERIALS
dried rose-heads
scissors
glue or glue gun
ready-made hop-vine or twig ring
sphagnum moss
potpourri
fir cones or woody material

ABOVE: *Although garlands are usually hung on a wall or door, they can be very effective as a table decoration, provided that they are not too large. Check that there are no pieces of wire sticking out from the back.*

1 Steam the heads of the roses to improve their appearance if necessary. Cut off the stems of the roses and glue the heads to the ring, some in pairs and others as single roses. Try to achieve a good balance. Next, glue hanks of moss to the ring in the gaps between the roses.

2 Now apply generous quantities of glue directly on to the ring and sprinkle on handfuls of potpourri, to cover the glue completely. Finally, add the fir cones or woody items, gluing them on to the ring singly or in pairs. Keep checking that all the material is well spaced. Work on the garland in sections and move the base ring around as you finish decorating each part.

RIGHT: *Try to keep the flowers and ingredients of this garland light and delicate. No decorative trimmings are really necessary but you could, perhaps, add a rustic trailing raffia bow.*

OLIVE OIL CAN ARRANGEMENT

2 Cut the dried roses so that they protrude about 10 cm (4 in) above the rim of the tin. Starting at the left-hand side of the tin, arrange a line of five tightly packed roses in the plastic foam from its front to its back. Continue arranging lines of five roses parallel to the first and closely packed across the width of the tin.

An old olive oil can may not be the first thing to spring to mind when considering a container for your dried flower arrangement, but the bright reds, yellows and greens of this tin make it an attractive option.

Since this container is so striking, the arrangement is kept simple, using only one type of flower and one colour. This creates an effective contemporary display.

MATERIALS
1 block plastic foam for dried flowers
knife
small rectangular olive oil can
scissors
40 stems dried 'Jacaranda' roses
raffia

ABOVE: If you come across a nice container, however unlikely, remember it may be just right for a floral display. If you are using dried flowers it does not need to be watertight.

1 Cut the plastic foam to fit snugly in the olive oil can, filling it to 2 cm (¾ in) down from its rim.

3 Continue adding lines of roses, until the roses are used up. Then take a small bundle of raffia about 3 cm (1¼ in) thick and twist it to make it compact. Loosely wrap the raffia around the stems of the roses just above the top of the tin and finish in a simple knot.

$\mathcal{S}$PRINGTIME CANDLE BOX

ABOVE: *Decorated candle boxes make ideal table centrepieces, which do not take up much room.*

This is a way of using gift boxes that are just too good to throw away. In this arrangement, an oval box is used. The candle shown is an option; a bigger box may need more than one candle to give the finished display a balanced look.

MATERIALS
glue gun
selection of leaves
box
scissors
1 block plastic foam for dried flowers
knife
candle
2 bunches miniature pink roses
florist's wires
sphagnum moss
raffia

2 Using the knife, trim the foam block to the size of the box. Apply glue to the base of the foam block and push it firmly into the box. Try to create a good, tight fit; this will help to ensure that the box keeps its shape.

4 Trim the roses so that the finished length will allow around 3 cm (1¼ in) to be pushed into the foam, and around 5 cm (2 in) above the leaves. Insert the roses around the outside edge, spacing them to cover the whole surface. Leave space around the candle, so that there is no risk of the flowers burning. Cut short lengths of wire and bend them double into U-shaped pins, to attach the moss. Fill any space with moss. Trim the moss around the candle.

1 Spread a little glue on the back of each leaf and press each one of them firmly on to the side of the box. If the leaves are not large enough to cover the depth of the box, start the first row of leaves at the top and cover the bottom of the previous row with the next. Place the top row of leaves so that they extend well above the lip of the box. Carefully wipe away any excess glue.

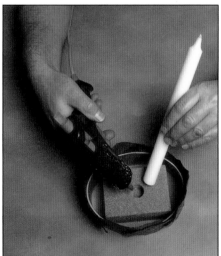

3 When the glue has dried, push the candle firmly into the foam in the centre of the box to make a hole. Then remove the candle and put a small blob of glue in the hole. Put the candle back into the hole, making sure that it is straight. The glue will ensure that the candle is safe. The candle stub should come out easily if it is twisted gently; remember to glue the new candle in.

5 Tie raffia around the outside of the box.

WARNING: Never leave burning candles unattended.

ROSE AND STARFISH WREATH

ABOVE: *The construction of this wreath involves some wiring but is otherwise straightforward.*

2 Cut the stems of the rose-heads to about 2.5 cm (1 in) and put glue on their stems and bases. Push the glued stems into the plastic foam, to form a ring around its outside edge, on top of the starfish. Working towards the centre of the ring, continue forming circles of rose-heads until the ring is covered, apart from a gap for the ribbon.

*T*he design of this visually simple wall decoration involves massing a single type of flower and framing them with a halo of geometric shapes, in this case, stars. The prettiness of its soft peach colours makes it suitable for a bedroom wall; if you are putting it in a bedroom, it is nice to sprinkle it with scented oil.

MATERIALS
10 small dried starfish
florist's wires
scissors
glue
13 cm (5 in) ring plastic foam for
    dried flowers
45 heads peach-coloured dried roses
velvet ribbon

1 Double-leg mount the starfish as an extension of one of their arms, with a florist's wire. Cut the wire to about 2.5 cm (1 in) and apply glue to both the tip of the starfish arm and wire. Push the wired arm into the out-side edge of the plastic foam ring. Position all the starfish around the ring. Leave a gap of about 3 cm (1¼ in) for attaching the ribbon.

3 Pass the ribbon through the centre of the ring and position it so that it sits in the gap between the roses and starfish, to cover the foam. This can be used to hang up the wreath or just tied in a bow for decoration.

ᴀ CROWN OF ROSES

There are many containers in the average household which, because of their colour, shape or material content, are suitable for a flower arrangement. This display was inspired entirely by the small crown-shaped, brass candleholder in which it is arranged.

An elevated position on, for example, a mantelpiece, would be perfect for such a small, neat display. Indeed, it could be used as a wedding-cake decoration.

MATERIALS
knife
1 block plastic foam for dried flowers
crown-shaped candleholder
scissors
15 stems poppy seed-heads
20 stems dried pink roses

ABOVE: *Making the display is straightforward and the method is applicable to any arrangement in a similarly small container.*

1 Cut a piece of plastic foam so that it can be wedged firmly into the candleholder, and sits about 2 cm (¾ in) below its top edge.

2 Cut the stems of the poppy seed-heads to 9 cm (3½ in) and push them into the foam, distributing them evenly to create a domed shape.

3 Cut the dried rose stems to 9 cm (3½ in) and push them into the foam between the poppy seed-heads, to reinforce the domed outline.

ROSE AND LAVENDER BASKET

This formal structure makes good use of three popular ingredients – roses, lavender and moss – and displays them to their best advantage in concentric rising patterns. Even stalks and waste leaves are used to dramatic effect. For this project, the basket was specially created from two rings fixed together with wire lengths – but a standard shallow round basket would work just as well.

MATERIALS
1 block plastic foam for dried flowers
knife
round basket
sphagnum moss
florist's wires
1 bunch dried lavender
scissors
about 25 stems dried red roses

1 Cut the foam to fit the basket and push in firmly. Make sure that the foam goes right to the edge and to the top of the basket.

2 Fix hanks of moss to the edge of the foam, so that it overlaps the top edge of the basket. Use florist's wires, bent double into U-shaped staples, to secure the moss in place.

3 Cut about 10–16 cm (4–6 in) off the bottoms of the lavender stalks. Wire them together at one end into even-size bunches, about 10 stalks per bunch. Press these in a circle into the foam, just inside the moss.

4 Wire up bunches of whole lavender in the same way, ensuring that they are of even height and that the flowers are level. Press carefully into the foam, to form an inner circle within the stalks, leaving a central circular space ready for the roses. Trim the roses and then wire into bunches of 2–3 flowers and insert into the centre.

RIGHT: This staggered raised circle structure is well suited to a number of different ingredients – apricot roses and dried grasses, for instance, could be just as pleasing. When adding central roses, try to ensure that they are placed at an attractive angle, facing outwards, and that they retain as much of their foliage as possible. Ideally, when viewed from above, none of the foam should be visible through the flowers.

Jam Jar Decorations

Containers decorated with plant materials can be very attractive. This type of external embellishment usually conceals a large part of the container, so do not waste money buying special pots and vases, just look around the house for something with an interesting shape that you can use.

Here, three different types and sizes of jam jars are decorated for use as night-light holders but they could be used to store pens or bric-à-brac or even in the bathroom for toothbrushes, although the damp will accelerate the deterioration of the materials.

Working on this scale does not use a great deal of material and is an opportunity to use leftover items or materials in some way unsuitable for flower-arranging. Use your imagination to vary the type of container and the flower decorations.

WARNING: Never leave candles burning unattended.

MATERIALS
floral adhesive
3 different-shaped jam jars
10 skeletonized leaves
scissors
18 heads dried yellow roses
3 night-lights
1 bunch dried lavender

ABOVE: These decorations would make an unusual centrepiece for a dining table.

1 Apply adhesive to the sides of the tallest jam jar (about 12 cm (4¾ in) high) and stick five upward-pointing leaves around the jar, flush with its base. Higher up the jam jar, glue on a second layer of leaves, slightly offset from the first layer.

2 Cut the stems off four dried yellow rose-heads and glue them to the jar at four equidistant points around the top of its outer surface. Place a night-light in the jar.

3 Cut the stems off 14 dried yellow rose-heads, apply floral adhesive to the base of each head and stick them around the neck of a more squat jar. Put a night-light in the jar.

4 Apply adhesive to the outside of the third jam jar. Separate the lavender into single stems and stick them vertically to the side of the jar, so that the flower spikes project about 1 cm (½ in) above its rim. The flower spikes should be tight to each other, to cover the sides of the jam jar. Apply a second layer of lavender spikes lower down. Trim the stems projecting below the jam jar flush with its base. Place a night-light in the jar, or use it as a small vase.

DRIED ROSE-HEAD CANDLE RING

*S*mall cane rings can be obtained from good florists but you could work with a length of hay rope instead, rather like a mini garland. Although any small-headed flower would be suitable for these decorations, dried roses are the perfect material. When the colours fade, spray on a frosting of gold or white paint to make Christmas candle rings. If you plan to use the decorations on tall candlesticks, make sure that you start the flowers well down the sides of the cane or hay ring, or the base and workings may be visible at eye-level to anyone nearby.

MATERIALS
glue gun
sphagnum moss
small cane ring or hay ring
scissors
8 heads dried roses
dried bupleurum
candle

1 Glue a light layer of moss to the cane or hay ring, making sure no glue is visible (it is white when set).

2 Cut all the roses from their stems, leaving as little stalk as possible, and begin to glue them into place. Position the roses carefully so that you maintain a symmetry in the design, unless that is you are deliberately aiming for a random, unstructured look. It is easiest to work on one side of the ring and then the other, to make sure the balance is right.

3 After you have added the roses, begin to fill in the spaces between them, using glue to fix the bupleurum in position. As you work make sure that the hole left in the middle will be large enough to take the candle. Fill any remaining gaps with more strands of moss. Finally, insert the candle in the ring.

ABOVE: If you are using more than one shade or variety of rose on a candle ring, glue them in pairs of different colours and try to position the heads so that they are facing outwards.

ABOVE: This garland is made in the same way as the round candle ring, but you need a heart-shaped stay wire as your starting point.

WARNING: Never leave candles burning unattended.

PARTY TABLE-EDGE SWAG

This is just about the simplest possible swag to make but, used as a table-edge decoration hanging in short loops, it gives an impressive finish to a festive table. Conifer boughs are inexpensive to buy and are freely available at any time of the year. You may have a suitable tree in your own garden, or be able to beg some from a friend.

This design is not long-lasting; the conifer will soon dry, become brittle and lose its vibrant green colour. If the swags need to be made a few days before the event, hang them in a cool, dry, dark place; this will ensure that the conifer stays looking good and this way there is plenty of time for other preparations. For a really fresh look, steam the roses gently to open them up.

MATERIALS
rope
fresh conifer
florist's reel wire
pale pink dried roses
scissors

1 Cut the rope to the required length and make a loop at each end. Trim the conifer to short lengths and remove any thorns and lower foliage from the roses. Bind the conifer to the rope, covering it all the way round, with reel wire.

2 Continue this process, adding the pink roses in twos and threes, with a handful of conifer stems at short intervals. Pack the conifer fairly tightly to produce a thick swag.

BELOW: *Pale pink roses are used here for a summer party, but you could change the rose colour to give a different feel: red roses mixed with the conifer and used on a dark background would create a wintry look; for spring, pale yellow roses could be used.*

DRIED ROSE TUSSIE MUSSIES

These tussie mussies are made of small spiralled bunches of lavender-scented dried flowers. Embellished with embroidered and velvet ribbon bows, they have a medieval look.

ABOVE: These tussie mussies are easy to make, although, to achieve a satisfactory result, they will use a lot of material in relation to their finished size.

2 Add, in turn, stems of *Nigella orientalis*, lavender and rose to the central stem. Continue this sequence, all the while turning the bunch in your hand to ensure that the stems form a spiral. Hold the growing bunch about two-thirds of the way down the stems (the binding point).

MATERIALS
Tussie Mussie A:
scissors
20 stems dried red roses
1 bunch dried Nigella orientalis
1 bunch dried lavender
string
ribbon

Tussie Mussie B:
scissors
20 stems dried pink roses
half-bunch nigella seed-heads
half-bunch dried lavender
half-bunch dried phalaris grass
string
ribbon

1 To make Tussie Mussie A, on the right of the main picture, cut all the materials to a stem length of approximately 18 cm (7 in). Set out all the materials in separate groups for easy access. Start by holding a single rose in your hand and add the other materials one by one.

3 When all the materials are in place, secure the bunch by tying string around the binding point of the stems. Trim the bottoms of the stems so they are even. Tie a ribbon around the binding point and finish in a neat bow. (Follow the same method for Tussie Mussie B.)

AUTUMNAL ROSE BUNDLE

This small display is one of the easiest to make, although it does have a fair number of steps. Dried roses, especially yellow or orange ones, will keep their colour for a very long time, so this makes an ideal design to fill a dark corner. Any combination of dried materials can be used. Raffia always gives a display a country feel; for a smarter location, the arrangement could be trimmed with a fabric bow.

BELOW: These flame-like roses make the arrangement suitable for autumn but you could vary the colours to suit any season or colour scheme.

MATERIALS

1 cylinder plastic foam for dried
flowers
brown paper
glue gun
knife
florist's wires
pliers
scissors
about 12 stems dried orange or
yellow roses
cobra or similar leaves
sphagnum moss (optional)
raffia

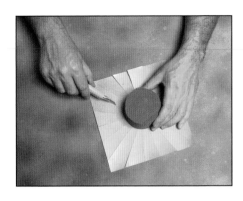

1 Place the foam cylinder in the centre of the brown paper and glue it in place. Cut from the edge of the foam to the outer edge of the paper, working all the way around at roughly 1 cm (½ in) intervals.

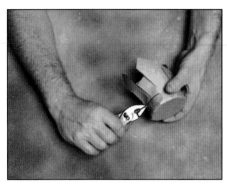

2 Fold the paper strips up. Wrap a florist's wire round the paper and the foam and twist the ends together.

3 Trim the paper in line with the top of the foam. Prepare and cut the rose stems, retaining as many leaves as possible. Starting in the centre, push them carefully one at a time into the foam.

4 Continue the process until the whole of the foam has been covered with roses. If more leaves are required in the display, wire some bunches together and add them to the foam.

5 Fix three to four cobra leaves around the base with florist's wires bent into U-shaped staples.

6 Make sure all the pins are at the same height. Wrap a wire around the leaves at the same level as the pins and twist the ends together.

7 If the roses had a limited number of leaves, fill spaces around the stems with moss. Trim the leaves at the base of the display with scissors.

8 Tie raffia around the base, covering all the fixings, and finish with a bow or simple knot.

DRIED ROSE TREE

Without doubt, roses are among the most extravagant of flowers. In the same way that the powerful scent of an old garden rose can unexpectedly halt passers-by, so dried roses can be used in topiary designs to stunning effect.

MATERIALS

self-hardening clay

plant pot

straight twigs firmly tied together at the ends

plastic foam ball

10-12 bunches dried roses

scissors

florist's wires

small-headed filler flowers, such as achillea ('Lilac Beauty'), Achillea ptarmica ('The Pearl'), Alchemilla mollis, bupleurum, marjoram, oregano or solidago

sphagnum moss

1 Place the ball of clay in the pot and push the prepared twigs into the clay. Secure the plastic foam ball on top of the twigs. Trim the rose stems about 7.5–10 cm (3–4 in) from the base of the flower-head. This length will vary, depending on the size you want the finished tree to be.

2 Wire small bunches of 3–4 flowers together. You can also add the greenery at this stage, by trimming leaves from the waste stems and wiring this to the flowers. To create a perfect round, the flowers must align at the same level.

3 Push the wired bunches one at a time into the foam ball. Work in turn on one side and then another, building a basic shape all around the sphere. When you have added 10–12 bunches and you are satisfied with the shape, start to fill the spaces in between with your chosen filler flower. Always support the foam ball with a hand on the opposite side to where you are working.

4 When all the flowers are in place, there may still be gaps. Moss is excellent for filling any small spaces, as its rich dark green provides a perfect background for the flowers. Cut short lengths of wire and bend them into U-shaped pins, to fix the moss in place. To finish, cover the base of the trunk and the clay in the pot with generous handfuls of moss.

ABOVE: *A tree of deep red and pale pink roses makes a stunning combination.*

ABOVE: *This rose tree has been sprayed with a fine coating of white paint to prolong its life.*

DRIED ROSE WREATHS

These two wall-hanging decorations show how massed dried flowers in strong contrasting colours can create a striking contemporary display.

One display couples white roses with blue globe thistles, the second red roses with yellow roses; but alternative materials can be used, provided all the flower-heads used are about the same size. Consider green *Nigella orientalis* with white roses, bleached poppy seed-heads with bright yellow helichrysums or blue sea holly with orange carthamus.

MATERIALS

Red and Yellow Materials:
scissors
34 stems dried red roses
33 stems dried yellow roses
glue gun
10 cm (4 in) diameter plastic foam ring for dried flowers
ribbon

Blue and White Materials:
scissors
25 stems dried white roses
26 small heads echinops (blue globe thistle)
glue gun
10 cm (4 in) diameter plastic foam ring for dried flowers
ribbon

RIGHT: *The wreaths are simple to make but will require a lot of material and a little patience to achieve the neat checkerboard patterns that characterize them.*

1 For the red and yellow wreath, cut the rose stems to about 2.5 cm (1 in). Around the outside edge of the plastic foam ring, form a circle of alternating yellow and red roses by gluing their stems and pushing them firmly into the foam. Leave a small gap in the rose circle for a ribbon. Inside the first circle, construct a second circle, offsetting the colours against the first ring.

2 Continue building circles of roses until the ring is covered. Pass the ribbon through the centre and around the gap on the plastic foam ring. Use the ribbon to hang the wreath or tie in a bow. Follow the same method for the second wreath.

DRIED FLOWER HAIR COMB

A decorated hair comb is a beautiful accessory for a special occasion and is particularly useful if the hair is worn up. This decoration in dried flowers is almost mono-chromatic, with creamy-white roses, silvery-grey eucalyptus, silvery-white honesty and soft green phalaris. Apricot-coloured dried starfish provide both colour and strong graphic shapes, which contrast with the softness of the flowers to create a stunning effect.

MATERIALS
scissors
7 heads dried yellow roses
9 heads dried phalaris grass
fine-gauge florist's wires
3 small dried starfish
9 short stems eucalyptus
5 heads dried, bleached honesty
florist's tape
plastic hair comb

ABOVE: *Subtle colours and strong shapes make a lovely, unusual hair ornament for a party.*

1 Cut the rose-heads and the phalaris to a stem length of 2 cm (¾ in), and double-leg mount them with florist's wire. Double-leg mount the small starfish with florist's wire. Cut two of the eucalyptus stems to a length of 6 cm (2¼ in) and the rest to about 4 cm (1½ in). Double-leg mount all the eucalyptus and individual heads of honesty with florist's wire. Cover the wired stems of all the materials with florist's tape. Create six units, two containing two roses, two with two phalaris and two with two eucalyptus stems, one at 6 cm (2¼ in) and one at 4 cm (1½ in), with the longer stem at the top of the unit.

2 Take two eucalyptus units and bind them together about 2 cm (¾ in) below the junction of the stems using florist's wire. At the binding point, bend each of the wired units away from each other, to form a straight line slightly longer than the length of the comb. Take all the units of rose and phalaris heads and bind them individually to the eucalyptus unit at the binding point. Bend each of them flat in the same way. Make all of these units slightly shorter than the eucalyptus.

ABOVE: This special-occasion hair comb is quite intricate to construct but can be made in advance of the event, and the materials are available all year.

3 Place an individual rose-head at the centre of the bound units with the top about 5 cm (2 in) above the binding point. This will be the focal flower. Position the starfish and the honesty around this central rose-head and secure at the binding point with florist's wire. Wire in the individual heads of phalaris and short stems of eucalyptus.

4 Next, separate the wire stems below the binding point into two equal groups of wires, bend them apart and back on themselves, parallel to the main stems. Trim the wires at an angle to thin them out, before covering each group of wires with tape to create two wire prongs.

5 Lay these two wire prongs along the flat back of the comb and tape into position, by passing the tape between the teeth in the comb and around the wire prongs. Do this all the way along the length of the comb until the decoration is securely attached.

ROSE AND LAVENDER POSY

A bouquet always makes a welcome gift, but a bunch of carefully selected and beautifully arranged dried flowers will long outlast fresh blooms, to become an enduring reminder of a happy occasion. The "language of flowers" interprets the meaning of lavender as "devoted attention" and the pink rose as a symbol of affection, so this posy should really only be made for a very special friend.

MATERIALS
florist's wires
12 large artificial or glycerined leaves
florist's tape
1 bunch dried lavender
1 bunch dried rose-buds
paper ribbon

ABOVE: *The soft colours of lavender and dried roses make this a striking arrangement.*

1 Fold a florist's wire one-third of the way along its length, to form a 15 cm (6 in) stalk. Attach a leaf to the top by its stalk and tape in place, wrapping the tape down to the end of the wire. Repeat to prepare 12 leaves.

2 Divide the lavender into several small bunches. Hold them together loosely, setting the bunches at an angle to each other to give a good shape. This will form the basic structure of the posy.

3 Taking a single rose-bud at a time, push the stems into the lavender, spacing them out evenly.

4 If desired, bind the posy with florist's wire at the binding point (where the stems cross) so it will keep its shape while you work. Then edge the posy with the wire-mounted leaves. Bind in place again.

5 Unravel the paper ribbon and use to bind all the stalks together tightly, covering the wire and the stalks completely. Finish off by tying the ends of the ribbon into a bow.

OPPOSITE: *Lavender and roses are a popular combination with flower arrangers.*

COUNTRY ROSE POT

This simple pot of rural roses has a pleasing dishevelled appearance. emphasized by the layer of hay attached to the outside of the terracotta pot. It is trimmed with a large loose raffia bow and would look wonderful on a traditional dresser or kitchen cabinet.

MATERIALS
knife
1 block plastic foam for dried flowers
terracotta pot
florist's reel wire
glue or glue gun (optional)
hay
scissors

1 bunch dried red roses
1 bunch dried poppy seed-heads
raffia

BELOW: To ensure that the roses retain their colour, keep the display out of direct sunlight. If the flowers or poppy heads become a little dusty, brush them clean with a dry paintbrush.

1 Cut the foam block with a knife to fit the pot and press firmly in. Tightly wrap reel wire 2–3 times around the pot near the top. If you have a glue gun, you could glue the wire to anchor it firmly to the pot.

2 Lay the pot on its side and wire on the hay in generous amounts. Do not worry if the hay is uneven, it will be trimmed later. As you add the hay, trap it tightly under the wire, or take the wire completely around the pot each time you add a new bundle.

3 When the pot is covered, tie the wire tightly. If you wish to be certain that the hay will not come off, glue around the pot over the wire and into the hay. Now trim the hay to expose the base of the pot. Pull off any loose strands. Do not trim the top but remove any straggly pieces. You should aim to get the hay looking fairly tidy, but do not spend too long fussing over it. The whole design will be transformed once you have started to add the flowers.

4 Separate the roses and poppies and wire them in groups of 3–4 into small bunches, although you might find it easier to work with individual, single stems. The heads need to show above the top of the hay collar, so remember to leave enough length on the stems to push into the foam. Fill the centre of the pot with the roses and poppy heads, making sure that you have a good balance of colour and form. Finally, tie a raffia bow around the pot to cover the wire that is fixing the hay. Try to make the loops of the bow well rounded and generous in size. Trim any unwanted raffia from the ends as necessary.

ABOVE: This variation of the Country Rose Pot shows how easy it is to achieve a different feel by changing the colour of the roses. Here country-style ingredients create a pretty, casual display. You could also replace the raffia bow with a fabric or paper one, for a more sophisticated look.

TRADITIONAL TIERED BASKET

This regimented formal design can be very effective and is one of the easiest for beginners to perfect. So long as you make sure that each layer of materials is the correct height, you should make a dramatic display, the loose and flowing ingredients combining well within the confines of a disciplined structure.

MATERIALS
knife
1 block plastic foam for dried flowers
rectangular basket
dried flowers and foliage such as
    wheat, lavender, roses
scissors or cutters
sphagnum moss
florist's wires

2 Lavender (wired into small bunches of 5–6 stems) is pushed into the foam directly in front of the wheat. Arrange the stems so that the lavender flowers come to just below the heads of wheat. Make sure the flowers are all facing the same way, to achieve symmetry.

3 Add the roses next, positioning them individually in front of the row of lavender. Try to keep as much foliage as space will allow, but be prepared to cut away a fair amount from each stem. Place the roses at slightly varying heights, so that each flower head is visible.

1 Cut the foam block to fill the basket and press firmly in. Start in the centre of the foam with the tallest ingredient (wheat in this case), wired into bunches of 8–10 stems. Pack the stems closely together, to achieve a good density. Check that the height balances visually with the size of the basket.

4 Complete the display by covering the foam at the base with generous handfuls of moss. Fix this in place with short lengths of florist's wires bent into U-shapes. Remember that fresh moss shrinks a little when it dries, so allow it to overhang the sides of the basket at this stage.

ABOVE: *This simple, structured display is most effective when created as a flat-backed piece, which can be placed against a wall or perhaps used to fill a fireplace during the summer months. It is also particularly well suited for window sills – the wheat will shield the flowers in front from strong sunlight so they will last for longer before their colours fade.*

DRIED ROSE BABY GIFT

What could be nicer for new parents than to receive a floral symbol of good luck on the birth of their baby? The whites and pale green of this dried-flower horseshoe make it a perfect, delicately coloured decoration for the nursery.

MATERIALS

14 heads dried white roses
42 heads dried bleached honesty
60 heads dried phalaris grass
scissors
silver reel wire
florist's tape
florist's wires
ribbon

2 Make a stay wire approximately 30 cm (12 in) long from florist's wire and florist's tape.

4 Form the stay wire into a horseshoe shape. Tape one wired end of the ribbon to one end of the stay wire. Tape one of the bows over the junction of the ribbon and stay wire, making sure it is securely in place.

1 Cut the rose stems, honesty stems and phalaris grass to approximately 2.5 cm (1 in) long. Double-leg mount the roses individually on silver reel wire, then tape. Double-leg mount the phalaris heads in groups of five, and the honesty in clusters of three, on silver reel wire. Tape each group.

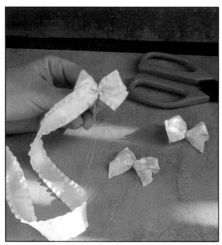

3 Form three small bows about 4 cm (1½ in) wide from the ribbon and bind them at their centres with silver reel wire. Cut a 30 cm (12 in) length of ribbon and double-leg mount both ends separately with silver reel wire. This will form the handle for the horseshoe.

5 Tape the flowers and foliage to the stay wire, to its mid-point, in the following repeating sequence: phalaris, rose, honesty. Tape a bow at the centre. Tape the last bow and the remaining ribbon end to the other end of the stay wire. Work the flowers in the same sequence to the centre point.

OPPOSITE: *While making the horseshoe is relatively time consuming, the effort will no doubt have created something of such sentimental value that it will be kept forever. An occasional dusting with a fine paintbrush will help to keep it looking good.*

MASSED ROSE STAR DECORATION

This display has a huge visual impact of massed colour and bold shapes with the added bonus of the delicious scent of lavender.

Built within a star-shaped baking tin and using yellow and lavender colours, the display has a very contemporary appearance. It would suit a modern interior.

MATERIALS
2 blocks plastic foam for dried
    flowers
knife
star-shaped baking tin
scissors
500 stems dried lavender
100 stems dried yellow roses

RIGHT: *This decoration is simple to make, although it does call for a substantial amount of roses.*

1 Cut the plastic foam so that it fits neatly into the baking tin and is recessed about 2.5 cm (1 in) down from its top. Use the tin as a template for accuracy when cutting the foam blocks.

2 Cut the lavender stems to 5 cm (2 in) and group them into fives. Push the groups into the plastic foam all around the outside edge of the star shape, to create a border of approximately 1 cm (½ in).

3 Cut the dried roses to 5 cm (2 in). Starting at the points of the star and working towards its centre, push the rose stems into the foam. All the heads should be level with the lavender flowers.

HEART AND FLOWERS

A heart-shaped dried-flower decoration with a traditional feel of the country. The construction of the heart could not be simpler and it will last a long time, if you do not hang it in direct sunlight. This is a lovely way to preserve the best of summer's harvest of roses to enjoy throughout the winter months.

MATERIALS

4 long florist's wires
florist's tape (optional)
florist's reel wire
hay
dark green florist's spray paint
clear glue or glue gun
wide red ribbon
narrow gold ribbon
large and small dried red roses
dried hydrangea heads
scissors

2 Using reel wire, bind hay all the way around the heart, to create a firm frame about twice the thickness of a pencil. Work around the heart at least twice with the reel wire, trapping as many loose ends of hay as possible. Cut off and tie the wire, and trim any loose ends of hay. Spray the whole frame dark green and leave it to dry.

3 Glue the end of the red ribbon to the bottom of the heart and wrap it around the frame. Repeat with the gold ribbon. Tie a bow at the top with a length of gold ribbon. Cut any stems from the roses and separate the hydrangea into florets. Glue the large rose-heads near the centre and surround them with hydrangea. Put the smaller rose-heads along the top.

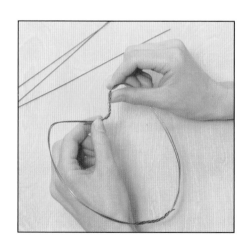

1 Form two pairs of florist's wires into a heart shape. The double thickness of the wire gives the arrangement better support. Tape or twist the ends together at the top and bottom of the heart.

ABOVE: *Roses are a symbol of romance* par excellence *and so what better way to preserve some beautiful garden roses than to combine them with that other emblem of romance: the heart.*

STARFISH AND ROSE TABLE DECORATION

This is an original decoration for a large church candle, using dried rose-heads and starfish. The result is a table-centre decoration with a seaside feel. This is a simple and quick decoration to make, but is very effective nonetheless.

WARNING: Never leave burning candles unattended.

MATERIALS
9 small dried starfish
florist's wires
church candle, 13 x 23 cm (5 x 9 in)
13 cm (5 in) ring plastic foam for
   dried flowers
scissors
reindeer moss
40 heads dried roses

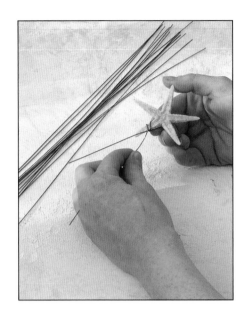

1 Double-leg mount all the starfish individually through one arm with florist's wires, to extend their overall length. Cut the wires to approximately 2.5 cm (1 in) in length and put the starfish to one side.

2 Position the candle in the centre of the plastic foam ring. Make 4.5 cm (1¾ in) long hairpins from cut lengths of florist's wires. Use these to pin the reindeer moss around the edge of the ring.

ABOVE: *The cream roses complement the colour of the candle and contrast is provided by the apricot colour and strong geometric shape of the small dried starfish.*

OPPOSITE: *Make sure that you replace the candle well before it reaches the level of the roses.*

3 Group the wired starfish into sets of three and position each group equidistant from the others around the foam ring. Push their wires into the foam to secure.

4 Cut the stems of the dried rose-heads to about 2.5 cm (1 in) and push the stems into the foam to form two continuous, tightly packed rings of flowers around the candle.

CHRISTMAS CENTREPIECE

Even the humblest materials can be put together to make an elegant centrepiece. The garden shed has been raided for this one, which is made from a terracotta flowerpot and wire mesh. Fill it up with red berries, ivies and white roses for a rich, Christmassy look; or substitute seasonal flowers and foliage at any other time of the year.

MATERIALS
knife
1 block plastic foam
18 cm (7 in) terracotta pot
about 1 m (39 in) wire mesh
beeswax candle
tree ivy
white roses
red berries
variegated trailing ivy

1 Cut the plastic foam to fit in the terracotta pot and soak it in water. Push the foam in the pot.

Place the pot in the centre of a square of wire mesh. Bring the mesh up around the pot and bend it into position. Position the candle carefully in the centre of the pot. Arrange tree-ivy leaves around the candle.

2 Add a white rose as a focal point, and arrange bunches of red berries among the ivy. Add more white roses, and intersperse trailing variegated ivy among the tree ivy.

WARNING: Never leave burning candles unattended.

OPPOSITE: *The wire mesh gives a strong, curving shape that is nevertheless light and airy. Its ruggedness prevents the traditional Christmassy elements from seeming clichéd.*

ROSE BUTTONHOLES AND CORSAGES

It used to be the fashion for gentlemen to present their ladies with an elaborate corsage of scented flowers to wear on a special occasion such as a grand ball. This custom is now mainly restricted to wedding guests wearing boring carnations with a sprig of asparagus fern as buttonholes. With imagination and a little skill and expenditure, though, it is quite possible to create some really attractive arrangements to wear for formal occasions, such as weddings or other special events. Traditional etiquette demands that ladies wear corsages with the flowers pointing downwards and gentlemen wear buttonholes with the flowers upright.

ABOVE: *Present buttonholes and corsages in tiny boxes protected by coloured tissue paper, to help them keep fresh until they are worn.*

Gentleman's Buttonhole

Materials

1 stem 'Ecstasy' rose
scissors
medium-gauge florist's wire
florist's tape
3 heads eryngium (sea holly)
3 heads lavender
2 ivy leaves

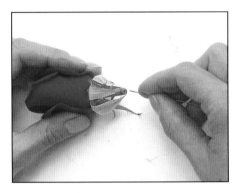

1 Assemble all the ingredients. Cut the stem off the rose about 1 cm (½ in) below the head. Push a small piece of florist's wire through the remaining stem up into the head. Check that the wire feels quite secure and not likely to become loose.

2 Pull the florist's tape so that it stretches and bind it around the stem and wire, sealing them together. Repeat this step, wiring and taping the eryngium stems and the lavender, to create two little bunches.

3 Wire the ivy leaves (see Lady's Corsage). Then arrange one individual flower with the ivy leaves so that the leaves form a flat back to the buttonhole. Ensure that the wires are completely covered.

4 To make the ivy leaves more stable, create a loop of wire at the back of the buttonhole to support each leaf.

Lady's corsage

Materials

medium-gauge florist's wire
2 stems 'First Red' roses
fine silver reel wire
2 large ivy leaves and 1 smaller one
florist's tape
2 sprigs cotoneaster berries
co-ordinating ribbon, preferably wired

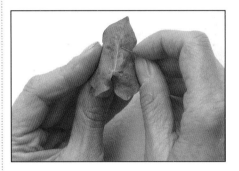

1 Wire the roses. Thread the fine wire through the main vein on each ivy leaf, leaving one long end.

2 Wrap the shorter wire around the stem. Wind the longer wire around the stem and other wire. Tape.

3 Add the roses and berries. Bind the stems and tie with a ribbon.

OLD-FASHIONED GARDEN ROSE CORSAGE

This delicate rose corsage would provide the perfect finishing touch for that special wedding or summer ball outfit. However, it has to be remembered that old-fashioned garden roses are really only available in the summer months.

MATERIALS

8 stems rose leaves

scissors

3 heads roses, graded thus: in bud, just open, fully open

3 small vine leaves

florist's silver wires

florist's tape

1 Cut the stems of the rose leaves to the following lengths: two at 6 cm (2¼ in), two at 4 cm (1½ in), four at 3 cm (1¼ in). Cut the rose-head stems to 4 cm (1½ in). Remove lower foliage and any thorns. Cut the vine leaf stems to 2.5 cm (1 in) and stitch-wire with florist's silver wire.

Make two "units" of rose leaves, each with one 6 cm (2¼ in) stem and one 4 cm (1½ in) stem. Make another unit using the two smaller rose-heads.

ABOVE: *Using just one type of flower, with its own foliage, and three individual leaves ensures the result is simple yet elegant.*

2 Hold one unit of rose leaves in your hand and place the unit of rose-heads on top, so that the leaves project slightly above the upper rose-head. Bind the units together with silver wire, 6 cm (2¼ in) below the lower rose-head.

Add the second unit of rose leaves lower and to the left of the first. Add the fully opened rose (the focal flower) with the top of its head level with the bottom of the rose above. Bind to the corsage.

Position the vine leaves around the focal flower and bind in place. Position the remaining individual rose leaves, slightly recessed, around the focal flower and bind in place.

3 Trim off the ends of the wires approximately 5 cm (2 in) below the focal flower and cover with tape. Adjust as desired.

ABOVE: *Commercially grown roses make an equally elegant corsage when garden roses are not available. Pick the colours carefully to complement the outfit.*

DRIED ROSE AND APPLE BUTTONHOLE

Dried flowers can also come into their own at weddings, though fresh ones are more usual. The advantages are that the bride can keep her flowers after the event and it may be a practical measure for a winter wedding, where fresh flowers are unavailable or expensive. This buttonhole is designed to be worn by a groom or best man and, unusually, incorporates fruit with the flowers and foliage.

MATERIALS

3 slices preserved apples
florist's wires
scissors
6 stems dried roses
6 short stems glycerined eucalyptus
1 small head dried hydrangea
florist's tape
silver reel wire

ABOVE: Apple slices give texture and a light touch to the decoration. Add a few drops of rose oil to give scent if you wish.

1 Double-leg mount the apple slices together on florist's wire. Trim each rose stem to 2.5 cm (1 in) and wire. Double-leg mount the roses in two groups of three. Leave a 5 cm (2 in) stem on the eucalyptus and hydrangea and double-leg mount on florist's wires. Tape all the elements.

2 Hold the rose-heads in your hand and place the apple slices behind. Then position the hydrangea to the left and bind together all the stems using silver reel wire. Position the eucalyptus stems to frame the edge of the buttonhole and bind with silver reel wire.

3 When all the elements are bound securely in place, cut the wired stems to a length of approximately 5 cm (2 in) and bind them with florist's tape. Adjust the wired components until you achieve the desired shape, not forgetting the profile.

YELLOW ROSE BUTTONHOLE

The bold choice of vibrant colours characterizes this stunning button-hole. The yellow roses and elaeagnus, the orange-red rose-hips and lime green fennel combine to produce a simple, visually strong decoration suitable for either a man or a woman.

MATERIALS

scissors

1 stem yellow rose

florist's wires

5 elaeagnus leaves, graded in size

florist's silver wires

15 rose-hips and leaves

1 head fennel

florist's tape

silver reel wire

pin

ABOVE: *As with all buttonholes, the construction involves wiring which is, of course, time-consuming. Make sure you leave plenty of time to create buttonholes on the day they are needed.*

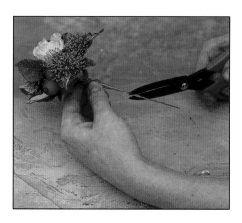

1 Cut the rose stem to 4 cm (1½ in), remove any thorns and wire. Stitch-wire all the elaeagnus leaves with silver wires. Group the rose-hips, on stems of 4 cm (1½ in), in bunches of five and wire with silver wires. Divide the head of fennel into its component stems and wire in small groups with silver wires. Tape all the wired elements.

2 Keeping the rose-head central to the display, bind the bunches of fennel and rose-hips around it, with silver reel wire. Bind the elaeagnus leaves to the arrangement with silver reel wire, placing the largest leaf at the back of the rose, the two smallest at the front, and two medium-sized leaves at the side.

3 Trim the wires to approximately 7 cm (2¾ in) and tape the wires with florist's tape. Look closely at the completed buttonhole, and, if necessary, bend the leaves down to form a framework for the rose and adjust the overall shape so that the back of the decoration is flat for pinning to the lapel.

CIRCLET HEADDRESS FOR A YOUNG BRIDESMAID

Although classic in its design, this bridesmaid's circlet head-dress is given a contemporary feel by the use of a rich colour combination not usually associated with traditional wedding flowers.

MATERIALS
9 heads deep red roses
9 small clusters apricot spray roses
8 small bunches rose-hips
scissors
florist's wires
9 small individual vine leaves
florist's silver wires
florist's tape
9 small bunches mint

ABOVE: *The small bunches of orange-red rose-hips give a substance to the fabric-like texture of the red and apricot coloured roses.*

1 Cut all the flowers to a stem length of approximately 2.5 cm (1 in) and remove any rose thorns. Wire the individual rose-heads with florist's wires. Stitch-wire the vine leaves with silver wire. Tape all the wired items.

2 Make a stay wire with florist's wires about 4 cm (1½ in) longer than the circumference of the head. Tape the wired flowers and foliage to the stay wire in the following repeating sequence: individual rose, mint, spray rose, vine leaf, rose-hips.

3 As you tape materials to the stay wire, form it into a circle. Leave 4 cm (1½ in) of the stay wire undecorated, overlap it behind the beginning of the circlet and tape securely together through the flowers.

DRIED FLOWER GARLAND HEADDRESS

This wedding headdress is made from dried materials in beautiful soft pale pinks, greens and lilacs with the interesting addition of apple slices. Apart from being very pretty, it will not wilt during the wedding.

MATERIALS
scissors
9 heads dried peonies with leaves
27 heads dried red roses
florist's wires
silver wires
silver reel wire
27 slices preserved apple
18 short sprigs ti tree
9 small clusters dried hydrangea
9 stems eucalyptus
florist's tape

1 Cut the peonies and the roses to a stem length of 2.5 cm (1 in). Double-leg mount the peonies with florist's wires and the roses with silver wires. Group the roses into threes and bind together using the silver reel wire. Group the apple slices into threes and double-leg mount them together with wire. Cut the sprigs of

ti tree, hydrangea clusters and eucalyptus to lengths of 5 cm (2 in) and double-leg mount with silver wires, grouping the ti tree and eucalyptus in twos. Cover all the wired stems with tape.

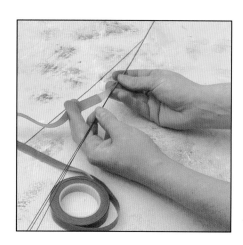

2 Have to hand the bride's head measurements. Make the stay wire on which the headdress will be built using florist's wires, ensuring its final length is approximately 4 cm (1½ in) longer than the circumference of the wearer's head.

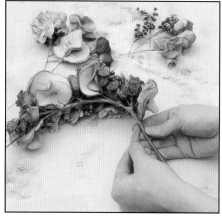

3 Position a piece of wired eucalyptus on one end of the stay wire and wrap florist's tape over its

stem and the stay wire, to secure them together. Then, in the same way, add in turn a hydrangea cluster, a group of roses, a peony and a group of ti tree, repeating the sequence until the stay wire is covered. Remember to leave the last 4 cm (1½ in) of the stay wire uncovered.

4 To complete the headdress, overlap the uncovered end of the stay wire with the decorated end and tape together with florist's tape, ensuring the tape goes under the flowers so that it is not visible.

OPPOSITE: *The bold nature of this headdress makes it particularly suitable for a bride.*

SIMPLE WEDDING BOUQUET

1 Strip all the flowers and foliage leaves and thorns which would be below the binding point, about a third of the way up each stem. Thorns should be neatly cut off so as not to damage the rose stems. Place a rose, a stem of mimosa and one of pittosporum in one hand to form the centre of the bouquet.

ABOVE: *The bouquet needs to stand in water for as long as possible before the big event, but dry the stems carefully before it is carried by the bride!*

2 With the other hand lay each subsequent stem at a 45° angle, always in the same direction. Turn the bouquet in the hand so that a spiral gradually develops. Hold the stems firmly at the binding point while adding new flowers.

A simple bunch of freshly picked flowers is the most traditional form of flower arrangement and its natural beauty is the fashion for most modern brides. Rather than the tortured wiring of every stem, the flowers are arranged in the hand, creating a spiral effect by placing the stalks in one direction. This style of arrangement, known as the hand-tied or continental bouquet, is very popular in Europe, particularly in the Netherlands where it was first developed. Unlike the old-fashioned flat or sheaf bouquets, in which all the stems are of differing lengths, the hand-tied bouquet is ready to go straight into a vase without any further arranging. The linear hand-tied bouquet is a very romantic arrangement, perfect for brides with long flowing dresses. It may be held either pointing downwards or in the curve of an elbow. Yellow and white flowers are synonymous with spring and several branches of mimosa add a sharp, sweet fragrance to the bouquet.

MATERIALS

5 stems commercially grown spray roses 'Yellow Dot'
5 stems commercially grown spray roses 'Tina'
5 stems mimosa
5 stems variegated pittosporum
5 stems pale yellow tulips 'Montreux'
5 stems white tulips 'Casablanca'
5 stems white anemone
5 stems trailing variegated ivy
string or raffia
scissors
white or pale yellow ribbon

3 Twist the string or raffia just above the hand and then take it up and around the stems and tie. With sharp scissors, trim all the stems to size, leaving a long slant at the end. Tie with ribbon.

HAND-TIED BOUQUET

ABOVE: *Brightly coloured ribbon that matches the flowers or the dress covers the raffia or string. This posy is easily kept in water before it is carried and may be made the day before the wedding, to allow some of the flowers to start to open.*

This jewel-coloured hand-tied bouquet is perfect for the less conventional bride or for those being married in winter who prefer bright tones. Make smaller versions for the bridesmaids. Flowers have tradition-ally been used to symbolize emotions and the use of the floral language was very popular in Victorian times when specific flowers were worn as a discreet form of communication between the sexes. The language of flowers is still observed by some brides when they choose their bouquet and, since the rose is associated with love, it is by far the most popular.

MATERIALS

7 *stems commercially grown rose*
  'First Red'
5 *stems commercially grown rose*
  'Ecstasy'
5 *stems commercially grown rose*
  'Leonardis'
5 *stems commercially grown rose*
  'Konfetti'
7 *stems orange ranunculus (turban*
  buttercup)
5 *stems viburnum*
5 *stems liquidambar (sweet gum)*
5 *stems cotinus (smoke bush)*
scissors
string or raffia
ribbon

THE LANGUAGE OF ROSES

Deep red rose *Simplicity and beauty*
Red rose *Eternal love*
Red rose-buds *Pure and lovely*

White rose *Truth*
Single rose *Simplicity*
White and red roses *Unity*

1 Prepare the ingredients by stripping off most of the rose leaves and all of those on the ranunculus and viburnum. Snip off all the rose thorns. Begin with a rose stem and lay a ranunculus stem over it.

2 Holding the stems upright, gradually add more stems to the bouquet at a 45° angle, turning the bouquet around in your hand as you work, to create the spiralling effect.

3 Once you are satisfied with the overall size and shape of the bouquet tie the stems together with string or raffia. Trim the stems and finish off with a coloured ribbon.

BRIDE'S VICTORIAN POSY WITH DRIED FLOWERS

*T*raditionally, the Victorian posy took the form of a series of concentric circles of flowers. Each circle contained just one type of flower, with variations only from one circle to the next. Such strict geometry gives formal-looking arrangements particularly suitable for weddings.

MATERIALS
scissors
11 heads white roses
18 heads pink roses
3 heads dried pink peonies
florist's wires
12 stems glycerined eucalyptus,
    approximately 10 cm (4 in) long
63 heads dried phalaris grass
12 clusters dried honesty, with 5
    heads in each cluster
florist's silver wires
12 small bunches dried linseed
10 small clusters dried hydrangea
florist's tape
silver reel wire
ribbon

1 Cut the roses and peonies to a stem length of 3 cm (1¼ in) and single-leg mount them on florist's wires. Cut the eucalyptus stems to 10 cm (4 in). Remove the bottom leaves, then wire as for roses and peonies.

Double-leg mount the phalaris grass and honesty heads on silver wire in groups of five. Single-leg mount these groups on wires to extend their stem lengths to 25 cm (10 in). Repeat the process with groups of linseed and hydrangea. Tape all wired elements with florist's tape.

2 Arrange the three peony heads around a white rose head. Bind together with silver reel wire, starting 10 cm (4 in) down the stems.

3 Rotating the growing posy in your hand, form a circle of pink rose-heads around the peonies and bind to the main stem. Around this, form another circle, this time alternating white rose-heads and clusters of hydrangea, and bind. Each additional circle of flower-heads will be at an increasing angle to the central flower, to create a dome shape.

4 Next add a circle of phalaris grass to the posy, followed by a circle of alternating honesty heads and linseed. Bind each circle with silver reel wire at the binding point as it is completed.

5 Finally, add a circle of eucalyptus stems and bind with tape. The eucalyptus leaves will form a border to the posy and cover any exposed wires underneath.

6 To form a handle, place the bundle of bound wires diagonally across your hand and trim off any excess wires. Tape with florist's tape and cover the handle with ribbon.

YELLOW ROSE BRIDESMAID'S BASKETS

ABOVE: *The flowers are secured in plastic foam and will remain lovely and fresh, for the bridesmaid to take away and keep after the wedding.*

2 Clean the leaves from the bottom 3 cm (1¼ in) of the birch stems. Arrange them in the plastic foam, creating an even, domed outline.

*T*hese arrangements will keep young bridesmaids happy on two counts: first, they are easier to carry than posies and, second the simple bright colours are such fun – sunshine yellow roses and lime green fennel in a basket stained orange-red.

MATERIALS

For each basket you will need:
half-block plastic foam
knife
1 small basket, plastic-lined
florist's adhesive tape, if necessary
scissors
30 stems birch, approximately 10 cm (4 in) long
10 stems yellow roses
5 stems fennel
raffia

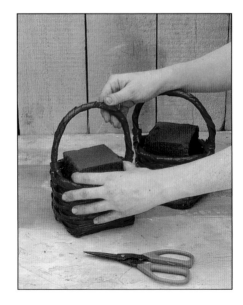

1 Soak the plastic foam in water and cut it with a knife to wedge firmly in the basket. (If you are using a shallow basket, you may need to secure the foam in place with florist's adhesive tape.)

3 Cut the roses and fennel to a stem length of 8 cm (3¼ in) and remove any thorns. Distribute evenly throughout the birch stems.

4 Tie a raffia bow at the base of the handle on both sides and trim to complete the display.

YELLOW ROSE BRIDESMAID'S POSY

A posy made from slim-stemmed materials has a narrow binding point which makes it easier to carry. This posy uses such materials in a simple but striking combination of yellow roses, lime green fennel and delicate green birch leaves.

MATERIALS

20 stems yellow roses

scissors

5 stems fennel

15 stems birch leaves

twine

raffia

ABOVE: *Easy to make as a hand-held, spiralled bunch and finished with a natural raffia bow, this posy would be a delight for any bridesmaid to carry and enjoy.*

1 Strip all but the top 15 cm (6 in) of the rose stems clean of leaves and thorns. Split the multi-headed stems of fennel until each stem has one head only. This makes them easier to handle and visually more effective in the posy. Strip all but the top 15 cm (6 in) of the birch stems clean of leaves.

2 Holding one rose in the hand, add individual stems of fennel, birch and rose in a continuing sequence, all the while turning the bunch to spiral the stems. Continue until all the materials are used.

3 Tie the posy with twine at the binding point – the point where the stems cross. Trim the bottom of the stems to leave a stem length of approximately one-third of the overall height of the finished display. Complete the posy by tying raffia around the binding point and finishing with a bow. Finally, trim the ends of the raffia.

Index

A

Apricot roses and pumpkins, 38
Autumnal rose bundle, 62, 63

B

Bride's Victorian posy with dried
  flowers,
  92, 93

Buttonholes
  and corsages,
  82-86

C

Celebration table decoration,
  42, 43
Christmas centrepiece, 80
Circlet headdress for young
  bridesmaid, 87
Containers for cut flowers,
  13, 24, 25
Containers, roses in, 24, 25
Country rose pot, 70, 71
Crowns of roses, 18, 19, 55
Cut roses, 8, 9

D

Double-heart basket, 46
Double-leg mount, 14
Dozen roses, styling with, 30, 31
Dried flower garland
  headdress, 88
Dried flower hair comb, 66, 67
Dried rose and apple
  buttonhole, 85
Dried rose baby gift, 74
Dried rose tree, 64
Dried rose tussie mussies, 61
Dried rose wreaths, 65
Dried rose-head candle ring, 59
Drying roses, 10, 11

E

Equipment, 12

G

Gentleman's buttonhole, 83

H

Hand-tied bouquet, 91
Heart and flowers, 77
Heart-shaped rose wreath, 45

J

Jam jar decorations, 58

L

Lady's corsage, 83

M

Massed rose star decoration, 76
Miniature roses, 40, 41
Mother's day basket, 28

O

Old-fashioned garden rose
  arrangement, 20
Old-fashioned garden rose
  corsage, 84
Old-fashioned garden rose
  posy, 34
Olive oil can arrangement, 51

P

Party table-edge swag, 60
Posies, tying, 15
Posy, tied, 26

R

Rose and fruit basket, 36
Rose and herb basket, 37
Rose and lavender basket, 56

Rose and lavender posy, 68
Rose and potpourri garland, 50
Rose and starfish wreath, 54
Rose-head, wiring, 15
Ruby wedding display, 21

S

Simple pot of roses, 48, 49
Simple wedding bouquet, 90
Single leg mount, 14
Small fresh rose Valentine's
  ring, 17
Springtime candle box, 52, 53
Starfish and rose table
  decoration, 78
Stay wire, 14
Steaming roses, 11
Summer gift basket, 27

T

Table arrangement with fruit and
  flowers, 32, 33
Table styling, 22
Topiary rose tree, 35
Traditional tiered basket, 72

V

Valentine terracotta pots, fresh, 16
Valentine's heart circlet, 44

W

Wiring cut roses, 14, 15

Y

Yellow rose bridesmaid's
  baskets, 94
Yellow rose
bridesmaid's
  posy, 95
Yellow rose
buttonhole, 86